RISKY
BUSINESS

RISKY BUSINESS

Taking and Managing Risks in Library Services for Teens

Linda W. Braun, Hillias J. Martin, and Connie Urquhart
For the Young Adult Library Services Association

American Library Association
Chicago 2010

ALA Editions purchases fund advocacy, awareness, and accreditation programs for library professionals worldwide.

The 2009–2010 president of the Young Adult Library Services Association (YALSA), **Linda W. Braun** is an education technology consultant with LEO: Librarians & Educators Online. She provides training and consulting to schools, libraries, and other educational institutions on how to integrate technology successfully. She is also an adjunct faculty member at Simmons College Graduate School of Library and Information Science, where she teaches courses on Web development and teen services. Linda has written books for ALA Editions, Neal-Schuman, Libraries Unlimited, and Information Today. She is also a TAG Team Tech columnist for *Voices of Youth Advocates,* and was blog manager for YALSA from 2006 through 2009.

Hillias "Jack" Martin began working in libraries at the age of thirteen when his mom volunteered him to work for his local public library in Cornelia, Georgia. Since then he has worked in Athens, Georgia, and in Providence, Rhode Island, leading him to his current position as assistant director for public programs and lifelong learning for children, teens, and families at the New York Public Library. He's an adjunct professor at Queens College and Pratt Institute, and is the coauthor of *Serving Lesbian, Gay, Bisexual, Transgender and Questioning Teens: A How-To-Do-It Manual for Libraries.* He lives on the Upper East Side of Manhattan with his husband and two bad cats.

Connie Urquhart is teen services coordinator for the Fresno County Public Library System, where she provides services to teens in all communities within Fresno County, California. She received her MLIS from the University of Washington's Information School and has presented workshops on booktalking, school and public library partnerships, and technology. An active YALSA member, Connie has served on several committees and task forces and is also a YALSA blogger. This is her first book.

Printed in the United States of America

15 14 13 12 11   5 4 3 2 1

While extensive effort has gone into ensuring the reliability of the information in this book, the publisher makes no warranty, express or implied, with respect to the material contained herein.

ISBN-13: 978-0-8389-3596-5

Library of Congress Cataloging-in-Publication Data

Braun, Linda W.
  Risky business : taking and managing risks in library services for teens / Linda W. Braun, Hillias J. Martin, and Connie Urquhart for the Young Adult Library Services Association.
    p.   cm.
  Includes bibliographical references and index.
  ISBN 978-0-8389-3596-5 (alk. paper)
  1. Young adults' libraries--United States. 2. Young adult services librarians--United States. 3. Libraries and teenagers--United States. 4. Teenagers--Books and reading--United States. 5. Young adults' libraries--Collection development. 6. Young adults' libraries--Activity programs. 7. Young adults' libraries--Information technology. 8. Risk-taking (Psychology) 9. Risk-taking (Psychology) in adolescence. I. Martin, Hillias J. II. Urquhart, Connie. III. Young Adult Library Services Association. IV. Title.
  Z718.5.B68 2010
  027.62'6--dc22

Book design in Bell and Bell Gothic by Karen Sheets de Gracia

♾ This paper meets the requirements of ANSI/NISO Z39.48-1992 (Permanence of Paper).

ALA Editions also publishes its books in a variety of electronic formats. For more information, visit the ALA Store at www.alastore.ala.org and select eEditions.

CONTENTS

Acknowledgments   *ix*
Introduction: A Risky Theme   *xi*

1 / **The What and Why of Risk Taking in Teen Services** *1*

2 / **Risk-Worthy Collections** *15*

3 / **Risk-Worthy Collections: What Authors Have to Say** *35*

4 / **Risks in Programming: A Necessity** *45*

5 / **Technology: A Risk Worth Taking** *61*

6 / **Selling Risk to Administration and Colleagues** *77*

7 / **Risky Career Moves** *87*

8 / **Teens as Risky Role Models** *99*

APPENDIXES

A   Meet the Risk Takers   *105*
B   Risky Decision Making: Assessing Risk Readiness   *109*
C   Risky Decision Making: Is This a Risk Worth Taking?   *113*
D   Forty Developmental Assets for Adolescents Ages
     Twelve to Eighteen   *117*
E   Resources That Support Smart Risk Taking   *121*
F   YALSA White Papers   *125*
G   Young Adults Deserve the Best: YALSA's Competencies for
     Librarians Serving Youth   *139*

Index   *145*

ACKNOWLEDGMENTS

We would never have thought to write this book without the inspiring conversations of the 2009–2010 YALSA Presidential Task Force. Frances Jacobson Harris, Lisa Lindsay, Jamie Mayo, and Becky Mazur were an energetic and idea-filled group for us to work with, and a lot of the original ideas for this volume came straight from the discussions we had with them.

The risk-taking librarians who filled out our survey online and talked to us via e-mail are also an amazing group of people. You can read more about these librarians throughout the book and read more of what they have to say in appendix A.

Four great young adult (YA) authors—Ellen Hopkins, Barry Lyga, Lauren Myracle, and Alex Sanchez—were kind enough to tell us their risk stories, several of which made us *verklempt* as we read about their commitment to taking risks in order to support the needs and interests of teens.

The YALSA Blog was an incredible resource as we researched this book, and many blog authors are quoted in the pages. Thanks to all of the YALSA bloggers for the time and commitment they put into getting out content to the wide array of readers that check out the blog on a regular basis.

It's clear from the work of the librarians and authors who are quoted within these pages that there is a lot of risky business going on in libraries today.

INTRODUCTION
A Risky Theme

Librarianship is a risky profession. Who knew?

The idea for this book is the result of several discussions of members of YALSA's 2009–2010 Presidential Advisory Task Force.[1] This group worked to develop the theme and programming for the presidential year of one of this book's authors, Linda W. Braun. Continually the discussions of the group focused on two ideas. One was that librarians often struggle with trying things out, admitting that their efforts weren't as successful as originally hoped, and using what was learned from a trial project in order to improve a program or service. This ended up being called the "I F@&!d up and then I fixed it" theme among task force members.

The second theme, labeled "Risky Business," centered on the idea that much of what a teen librarian has to do in her job is risky. The Presidential Advisory Task Force talked about materials in the collection, such as adding books with explicit sex scenes. They discussed programs that might be risky, such as giving teens the chance to manage a program for younger children. And they talked about the risks inherent in almost any spontaneous conversation a librarian and teen have. For example, how does a librarian respond to a teen who asks about the best way to handle an abusive relationship?

It was clear too to task force members that the "I F@&!d up and then I fixed it" philosophy is a component of librarian risk taking. Librarians are very happy to provide best practices and show how their programs, services, collections, and so forth succeed. But when do we see published and lauded examples of worst practices? Very rarely, and that's because it's pretty risky to say to the world, "I F@&!d up." But talking about worst practices is a risk worth taking, because it can actually help librarians be even more successful in their own libraries. The best practices show what works; the worst practices show how to get to what works. The combination is what helps librarians succeed.

The Risky Business theme struck a strong chord with members of the task force because it was clear through their discussions that so much of what a teen librarian does every day includes an element of risk. And the group realized that sometimes, because of a fear of risk taking, librarians don't always take the extra step in order to serve teens as well as they should. With that, the YALSA 2009–2010 presidential theme was launched and a component of that theme is this book.

WHAT'S IN A BOOK ABOUT THE BUSINESS OF RISKY TEEN SERVICES

Risky Business is task force members Connie, Jack, and Linda's way of ferreting out many of the risky topics that were discussed during conversations among the full group. It also gives librarians and authors who are risk takers the chance to tell a bit about their endeavors—specifically in this book:

Chapter 1 provides an overview of the many reasons why teen librarians should be risk takers. It includes information on why teens need to have opportunities to see adults as risk takers, how risk taking can help teens to grow up successfully, how risk is an important part of teen advocacy, and how innovation in teen services requires a commitment to risk.

Every day librarians purchase materials for their collections that are no doubt risky. A key feature of chapter 2 is a set of risky collection development scenarios with suggestions for how to successfully manage the risk within the areas covered. There is even a breakdown of the level of risk involved within each scenario with low-, medium-, and high-risk options for different collection development situations.

Librarians definitely need to be willing to take risks when selecting materials for their collections. But authors who write books for teens take their own risks when developing plots, themes, and characters that might be controversial. Four authors (Ellen Hopkins, Barry Lyga, Lauren Myracle, and Alex Sanchez) contributed to chapter 3 about the risks each has taken when writing for teens. The authors also discuss why it's important for librarians to purchase risky materials for their collections.

The opening paragraph of chapter 4 states, "Programming for teens in libraries is a great way to tie all aspects of teen librarianship into one (or two, or three, or more) amazing event. It encompasses nearly all the work teen librarians do: talking with teens, building collections, mobilizing staff expertise, planning, advertising, and more." To create amazing events with and for teens, librarians need to be smart about taking risks but not shy away from them. Learn how to do that in this chapter.

Because many librarians did not grow up with technology as a part of their day-to-day lives, sometimes integrating any technology into services for teens can seem very risky. Chapter 5 offers guidance on risk taking with social media, technology collaborations, and filtering. It also provides information on how to include technology components into traditional services, such as booktalks, information literacy instruction, and book discussion groups.

Sometimes the reason why librarians don't take teen services risks is that working with administration to gain needed support can be scary and a risk in itself. Chapter 6 examines barriers related to selling risk to administration and how to take positive steps in effectively gaining administrative support.

The authors of *Risky Business* have taken risks in their careers. In chapter 7, each tells his or her risky stories and provides ideas on how to be smart when considering career moves that might very well be risky.

In 2004, Students Against Destructive Decisions reported that teens who take positive risks are more likely to steer clear of negative risk taking.[2] Read chapter 8 to learn more about why it's important to give teens the opportunity to be risk takers and read about teens who have been successful as risk takers.

Each chapter includes quotes from librarians who have taken risks as a part of their service to teens.

The appendixes of *Risky Business* include decision-making tools to help determine what is needed to begin smart risk taking in the library. The resource list highlights articles and websites about risk in libraries, risk management, and teens and risk taking. In addition, the appendixes offer YALSA's competencies for serving youth and YALSA's white papers, which discuss the importance of teen literature, the need to include young adult services in library school curricula, the need for dedicated teen space in public libraries, and the need for dedicated teen services staff in public libraries.

IN THE END

The authors hope that readers of this book can use the contents to begin taking smart, successful risks in library teen services. But perhaps more than that, the authors hope readers will be ready, willing, and able to stand up to the challenges of risk taking. Library teen services is risky business. If the librarians who serve teens aren't willing to be risky, then teens are not being served in the way they deserve.

NOTES

1. Members of the 2009–2010 Presidential Advisory Task Force were Frances Jacobson Harris, librarian, University Laboratory High School (Urbana, Illinois); Lisa Lindsay, teen librarian, Fresno County (California) Library; Jack Martin, assistant director for public programs and lifelong learning, the New York Public Library; Jamie Mayo, Kansas City (Missouri) Public Library; Becky Mazur, librarian, South Hadley (Massachusetts) High School; and Connie Urquhart, teen services coordinator, Fresno County (California) Library.

2. Glenn Greenberg and Deborah Burke Henderson. "Positive Risk Taking Cuts Alcohol and Drug Use Among Teens," SADD Teens Today, November 29, 2004, www.sadd.org/teenstoday/survey04.htm.

1

The What and Why of Risk Taking
in Teen Services

The word "risk" refers, often rather vaguely, to
situations in which it is possible but not certain that
some undesirable event will occur.

"Risk," *Stanford Encyclopedia of Philosophy*

That definition states very succinctly what makes the idea of taking risks frightening to many librarians. It's not easy to make a decision if that decision will lead to something unpleasant. Everyone prefers to make decisions that are certain to bring good consequences. For example, it's fairly easy to decide to help a teacher collect resources for an upcoming unit; the risks in doing that are most likely pretty minuscule. But it's more difficult perhaps to decide to have a conversation with teens in the library about decisions related to smoking, drinking, or sex. Those discussions can be pretty risky, as a teen librarian could worry that a parent, or administrator, would hear of the discussion and question its value within the library setting.

When working with teens in a library, however, risk is a natural and important part of the job. A librarian who doesn't take on the challenge of risk taking in teen services could very well not be serving the teen population successfully. As YALSA past president Michael Cart said in an interview about risk in teen services, "I think anybody who elects YA librarianship as a profession is demonstrating risky behavior."

An Interview with Michael Cart

Q. What did Risky Business for young adult librarians look like ten years ago?

A. It wasn't a pretty picture! In fact, I chose "Risky Business" as the theme for my 1997–98 YALSA presidential year to focus attention and action on redeeming young adults, young adult literature, and the profession of young adult librarianship from the risks that then threatened to overwhelm them. In articulating these risks in my first presidential message, I quoted then teen activist Danny Seo who, in his book *Generation React,* had written, "Have you noticed? Our generation faces problems that didn't exist when our parents were our age. So it's not surprising that many of us feel hopeless about the future." Some of us in the profession were also feeling a bit hopeless about serving the growing needs of teens, since no more than 11 percent of America's libraries then employed a young adult librarian. As for the literature, it had been pronounced "near death" as early as 1994 when YALSA held a preconference to examine the health and prospects for the future of this still young genre that seemed to be in imminent danger of extinction.[1]

Q. How do you think it's changed since? What does risk look like now?

A. The situation has changed dramatically for the better, especially for YA literature and YA librarianship. The literature, for the past ten years, has been enjoying a new golden age that shows every indication of continuing for the foreseeable future. Meanwhile YALSA became the fastest-growing division in ALA, while 51.9 percent of America's libraries now report having at least one full-time librarian devoted to providing young adult service, and teens seem to be taking advantage of this happy circumstance. In a recent Harris Interactive poll, four out of five teens reported being library users. Unfortunately, the teens themselves continue to lead lives that are no strangers to risk. According to the National Longitudinal Study on Adolescent Health, the main threats to adolescents' health are the risky behaviors they themselves choose. Lynn Ponton, author of *The Romance of Risk: Why Teenagers Do the Things They Do,* explains, "Adolescents define themselves through rebellion and anger at parents or other adults, engaging in high risk behaviors . . ." Happily, the incidence of many of these risky behaviors seems to be showing a gradual decrease.[2]

Q. What was the biggest risk you've taken as a young adult librarian?

A. Alas, I was never a young adult librarian; my professional career was spent as a library administrator who was an advocate for youth and youth services, and that's what led me to my involvement with YALSA and, subsequently, with young adult literature. It's my career as a writer and editor that has invited me to take risks, particularly as one who believes we must trust YAs with the truth, no matter how hard-edged. That's why I've tried to be an advocate for unsparing realism in YA literature. I've tried to be true to this in my own books, especially *Love and Sex: Ten Stories of Truth* and *How Beautiful the Ordinary: Twelve Stories of Identity,* both of which push the envelope in terms of the frankness of their sexual content.

Q. Have you heard of any risks from young adult librarians that made you raise an eyebrow?

A. I think anybody who elects YA librarianship as a profession is demonstrating risky behavior. The sad truth is that too many people continue to dislike and distrust teens and, by extension, those who advocate for them. After I retired in 1991, I spent some years consulting with libraries and library systems on YA service and the single most common problem I was asked to address was staff reluctance to deal with YAs.

Q. How are libraries aligning themselves to meet the risky needs of the teens who use them?

A. Following YALSA's lead, I would hope they are focusing on the needs and competencies of YAs instead of only their specific problems. They are also now routinely involving teens in every aspect of service and programming, from planning to execution. They are also developing new collections in new forms, formats, and technologies that change with the needs and habits of YAs. And, I would hope, they are embracing flexibility and being open to new ways of serving the always new needs of their teen populations. As YALSA's recently launched examination of service to older YAs in the later teens and early twenties suggests, libraries are also willing to redefine their service populations to conform with societal realities.

Q. How has risky business in young adult literature changed? What authors are taking the biggest risks now as opposed to ten years ago?

A. What a good question. For starters, the literature is much more mature and sophisticated in its content than it was a decade or so ago. And I'm not only speaking of a new candor in addressing previously taboo subjects such as sexual abuse, incest, and other edgy topics, but also a new willingness to embrace innovative narrative forms, experimental literary techniques, and character-driven (instead of plot-driven) content. Today's writers are showing a salutary willingness to trust their readers by challenging them with both topics and techniques. Four writers who I think best exemplify this kind of risk taking are M. T. Anderson, Adam Rapp, Philip Pullman, and Aidan Chambers.

Q. What advice would you give young adult librarians and library students who are taking or are about to take risks? What advice would you give their managers?

A. Talk with, not at, young adults. Be flexible, be fearless, and—believing in what you do—trust your instincts. As for managers: trust your staff and never forget that today's teens are tomorrow's community leaders and potential library advocates.

WHY TEEN SERVICES ARE AND SHOULD BE RISKY

That isn't to say that every risk a teen librarian might take is worth it. But it is important that teen librarians don't go into their work with an aversion to risk. Or that teen librarians don't go into the job thinking it's a nice, cozy, and safe line of work. Instead, teen librarians need to be open to the possibilities of risk and also know how to make good decisions about when to be risky—and when not to be.

WHO TEENS ARE

For many teens, every day is a risky proposition. There is risk in:

- standing up in front of class and presenting a project
- walking into a school social event or party outside of school
- getting up in the morning and deciding what to wear
- letting friends and family members know about sexual orientation
- talking about problems with friends, family, or other adults in the community

The Search Institute's Forty Developmental Assets (see appendix D) provide a good framework for what teens need to grow up successfully. Many of these assets point to the need for teens to learn how to take and manage risks to become successful adults. For example:

The *Boundaries and Expectations* asset includes the importance of *adult role models*. This speaks directly to the need of teens to have adults in their lives who can demonstrate smart and safe behaviors. Teens need to look at adults—say, a librarian—to see how to handle a situation that might be risky, and know how to react if confronted with a similar circumstance.

The *Positive Values* asset states that teens need to take responsibility for their own actions. This isn't something that teens naturally know how to do, although many adults think that it is. It can seem very risky to a teen to take responsibility for something that didn't go as planned. Teens therefore need opportunities to practice taking responsibility for their actions. They can do that in a variety of ways connected with the library, including managing a library card account, helping to select materials for the collection, and completing tasks as a part of a teen advisory board project.

The *Social Competencies* asset discusses resistance skills and a teen's ability to resist negative peer pressure and dangerous situations. It can be very risky for a teen to go against the crowd and resist what others are doing and suggesting that she do. Libraries can help teens to gain this asset and learn how to manage associated risks by providing materials that show how to resist peer pressure and activities that provide opportunities to practice taking these kinds of risks within a safe, librarian-managed environment.

For some teens, the library may be the only place in which it's possible to access answers to questions about relationships with the same or the opposite sex. The library might be the only place a teen can go to learn about how to be safe when using social media. Or the library may be the only place where a teen feels comfortable being part of a project in which his ideas are valued. It's important to give teens opportunities to gain assets by giving them the chance to take the risks necessary to do so. (See chapter 8 for more information on teens as risk takers.)

TEEN LIBRARIANS AS ADVOCATES

The authors of the article "Teen Risk Behavior," published by The Ohio State University Extension, state,

> As parents, mentors, and role models we are charged with helping teens navigate the complicated landscape of risks and their consequences. We must take this role seriously and make sure that they understand the impacts these behaviors can have on their life.[3]

Librarians definitely fall into that continuum of adults in the community that need to support teens in "navigating the complicated landscape of risk."

If a librarian working with teens is not able to help teens manage and learn about risks, is she really doing her job? What if a teen is trying to figure out how to tell his parents that he is gay? He goes to the library, hoping there is a novel about a teen like him. He wants to see how another teen managed this type of risk to figure out how he can move forward himself. If the library doesn't have any novels on the topic, what's the teen to do?

While members of the community might feel uncomfortable having materials related to sexual orientation in the collection, should they be the ones to decide what should and shouldn't be included? Do they understand the type of support teens need to make good decisions? Do they think that if a teen can read about sexual orientation in a library book, that they might have to answer a question a teen has about the "scary" topic? Is that a good reason not to provide teens what they need? Who gets to make that decision? It should be the teen librarian who is looking out for the needs of teens in the community first, while at the same time taking the risk and informing community members regularly about why materials are in the collection, how programs are organized, and when discussions are held. (See chapter 2 for information on building risk-worthy collections.)

ASSESSING THE RISK

Of course not all risks that a teen librarian might take to serve teens successfully are smart risks. And, sometimes, a risk might be worth taking, but the time isn't quite right to jump in and do it. It's therefore a good idea to consider these factors when deciding whether to take a risk:

> **Where does the risk come from?** Is it an internal or external risk? In other words, does the risk come from the possibility of going up against the views and ideas of coworkers or administrators (an internal risk)? Is this something that might be risky within the larger community of parents, teachers, and other authority figures (an external risk)? If it's an internal risk, ask, will taking the risk make the working environment nearly impossible to exist in? If an external risk, what will the impact be on overall community support of the library? It's important

to consider where the balance falls when thinking about the value of the risk you might take against the internal discomfort or changes in library community support. If the risk might lead to short-term difficulties but long-term gains, then it could be a risk worth taking.

Who will benefit from the risk? Is the risk something that all teens in the community will benefit from or will it be more of a risk that supports the needs of a small group? Even if it's a small group of teens who gain from the risk taking, is their benefit so great that the risk could be seen as meeting a large need? Because teens are a teen librarian's primary audience, if the risk benefits a large or small group of that audience, the risk needs to be taken seriously. If teens benefit while adults might freak out, consider the value of standing up for the teens and at the same time helping educate adults about the importance of taking risks to serve teens effectively.

What are the benefits of the risk? Will the risk help teens to be healthy and grow up successfully? Will the risk help the library move into providing contemporary services to teens? Will the risk help the library better inform the community about what the library is about and aims to achieve within the community? This is an instance where long-term thinking and big-picture planning should definitely come into play. If the risk under consideration might put the library or the teen librarian in the forefront of a controversy in the community in the short-term, but in the long-term provide the library with greater opportunities for serving teens successfully, maybe it's worth taking. Don't just think about the benefits today, tomorrow, and next week. Think about what the benefits are in six months, a year, or five years, and how those benefits might be turned into even greater opportunities for taking risks and making changes for teens in the community.

What would be the outcome of not taking the risk? If the risk isn't taken, who would lose out? Will the library be seen as unsupportive to teens in the community? Will teens use other resources and venues to get the information, programming, and services they need? As mentioned previously, remember that teens are the primary audience for library teen services. If not taking the risk means that they are not being served, is not taking that risk more risky than actually taking it? Don't be scared to take a risk if that fear is keeping teens from the best service the library can offer.

Along with considering these factors when determining whether to take a risk, it's also important to think about what to do to manage the risk once a decision is made. Here are some tips for managing risk:

Consider how to limit the risk: Maybe it's a good idea to start small and then build on the first small steps. For example, if implementing social media technology into programs and services is risky because of external concerns, then it might be smart to start with a limited scale project. This could be a project in which the librarian works with a small group of teens using a book service like Goodreads as a Web 2.0 platform for book discussion. As adults in the community see that the Web-based book discussion can be managed safely and successfully in the online social world, the project can be expanded to other social tools and with a larger group of teens.

Make sure to inform, educate, and communicate every step of the way: No matter what the risk is, make sure that all who might be concerned are kept up to date. Keeping something secret makes it seem like the risk is more risky than it actually might be. Being out in the open helps people understand that everything is under control and the project is well thought out.

PERCEIVED VS. ACTUAL RISKS

One thing that holds librarians back when considering risks in the workplace is a perceived sense of risk as opposed to a knowledge of what the actual risks are. For example, consider the librarian who thinks if she sponsors an anime club in the library, then her administration and community members will be up in arms. Because some people see anime as not much more than watching Saturday morning cartoons, she worries she'll get flack for starting the program at the library.

But this is only a perception of the librarian. She hasn't asked anyone about it. She hasn't brought the idea to the library director. She hasn't talked to parents whom she knows. She hasn't done any research; it's just something she feels in her gut.

These perceived risks are often the result of fears—and it's important that librarians not be taken in by these fears. There is a fear of bringing up a new program or service to administration because an administrator might say "no," and it's never pleasant to have an idea turned down. Or it could be frightening to bring the topic up because the administrator might ask questions that the librarian can't answer (which, of course, means it's important to do homework before presenting the idea to anyone). And it's scary to start something new that might not go as planned. The teens who promised to attend might not. The equipment for showing anime in the library meeting room might break. A parent might walk in while the program is going on and ask questions. It's true, any of these could take place. But how does the librarian know what the real risks of this program are without talking to people, doing research, and trying things out?

THE ONLY WAY TO BE INNOVATIVE IS THROUGH RISK TAKING

Often perceived risks, rather than actual risks, hinder librarians from serving teens as well as they should. In addition, focusing on perceived rather than actual risks also means librarians aren't as innovative in offering programs and services as they might be. But think about it. Isn't every new program or service a risky proposition? Of course, some are riskier than others, but whatever the innovation—starting a new book discussion group, changing the policy on the number of items a customer can check out at one time, creating a book review blog—change can be risky because it's not clear exactly what the outcome will be.

For some new programs and services, it's easy to take a chance. There might be a lot of teens asking for the new activity, so starting it is easily justifiable. Perhaps the library director says this is something we have to do, so it gets done. Those are situations that can be seen as very safe risk taking. But what about those times when it's not clear that starting something new is going to be successful or supported by the community and the library administration? That's when it's easy to make excuses to avoid taking a risk. But again, if the risk isn't taken, are teens being served successfully?

Imagine if a library provided the same services, programs, and collections to teens in 2010 as it did in 1950. Would that library really be meeting the needs of contemporary teens? And in the world of Web 2.0, handheld devices, and social networking, a library that doesn't take risks to support teens today is taking the chance that they won't be needed by teens of tomorrow. Perhaps in 1950 innovation and change could come slowly and risks could be minimized. But with all of the opportunities teens have today for finding information, connecting with others, and accessing fiction and nonfiction materials, the library that plays it safe risks losing its credibility and value in the community, and with teens specifically.

Wiktionary includes this definition of the term innovative: "Forward looking; ahead of current thinking." A librarian who is ahead of current thinking definitely needs to be risky. A librarian who serves teens successfully has to think ahead of everyone else to adequately prepare for the emerging needs of teens who live in a world filled with questions, physical and emotional change, and dynamic pop culture.

DON'T WORRY, BETA CAN HELP IN MANAGING RISKS

One of the attributes of the Web 2.0 culture is an understanding that a successful new product doesn't just drop from the sky. More and more businesspeople, educators, librarians, and others are realizing that to be successful, it's important to get feedback from users as a product or service is in development. Did you know that Google's Gmail service maintained a beta label for five years? That label helped users understand that it was a product under development and, as such, was going to change and grow over time. For librarians serving teens, it's possible to use this approach when taking risks in what the library offers.

Perhaps it's time to add urban lit to the library's teen collection. Teens ask for the materials, but the library administration and colleagues often raise concerns about the materials' language, sexual content, and violence. This is a perfect opportunity to sell the additions to the collection as a beta project. Tell the administration that it's okay to start small to find out how well the materials circulate and the kinds of feedback provided on the inclusion of urban lit in the collection.

It's not necessary to buy every urban lit title available to start the collection. Instead buy a few titles that are certain to be popular with teens. Gather feedback from the teens who check out the materials. After a short period of time, perhaps three months, show the administration the positive comments received about the materials and the circulation numbers (which one can assume are high) for the new additions. Include information about the cost of the materials and how those circulation figures demonstrate that the money is being well spent.

Once it's clear that the collection is successful, then consider expanding on what was originally purchased. Don't just focus on expansion, however; use the beta period as a way to find out what teens are interested in regard to urban lit and what titles and authors might be important to add once the beta period is over. The beta phase should demonstrate how successful the program, service, or collection is and it should also provide information for making changes as the project moves out of beta.

IT'S OK TO MAKE MISTAKES

The beta approach to new and improved programs and services provides librarians with the opportunity to make mistakes and fix them. Promote that new urban lit collection in the library as a beta project. Actively ask for feedback. And just as actively, let teens, administrators, colleagues, and community members know what you learned from the feedback and the changes that will be made as a result. Don't hide from needing to revise. Embrace it. Teens learn from making mistakes and so can you. Consider the beta approach as a way to say, "I messed up but then I fixed it." That sends the message that the library is regularly looking at what it does and how it does it. It sends the message that the library is willing to change to provide the best service possible. It sends the message that the library is willing to admit that sometimes things don't go as well as hoped and planned, but that doesn't mean the institution gives up. It just means that new approaches need to be considered.

If librarians are willing to take risks in teen services to innovate and serve the population successfully, then teens will know they have access to a library that is willing to serve their twenty-first-century needs and that they have access to a staff who is willing to stand up for those needs. Isn't that what libraries and librarians are supposed to do for the entire community?

NOTES

1. For a much more discursive discussion of all of these risk factors, see Michael Cart's *From Romance to Realism* (New York: HarperCollins, 1996).

2. For more information, see the National Risk Behavior survey, which the Centers for Disease Control conduct every two years among ninth through twelfth grades, www.cdc.gov/yrbss.

3. Kara Newby and Anastasia Snyder, "Teen Risk Behavior," *Family and Consumer Services Fact Sheet*, Columbus: The Ohio State University Extension, http://ohioline.osu.edu/hyg-fact/5000/pdf/5240.pdf.

2

Risk-Worthy Collections

Erin Downey Howerton told the authors about a past incident when her library asked her to select books from the teen collection that might be too mature for younger patrons and move those books to a new "older teen" section. She refused. Her thinking was, "If I agree to this, how long until there are no more books left in the regular teen collection?" Eventually, with the help of ALA's statement on labeling and content, Erin convinced her administration to see her point. A risk? Absolutely. Not only did Erin vocally disagree with her superiors; she took a stand to advocate for teens and their access to materials.

That's what collection development is all about—providing access to things like books, movies, music, video games, and information. A risky business in and of itself, the process becomes even riskier when the collection is for teens. Not surprisingly, it's also an area where librarians find themselves in the position of feeling afraid or defensive. This chapter will help assuage some of that fear and anxiety by breaking down the types of risk involved in collection development and why it's important to consider jumping into risky collection development.

But before discussing risk taking with teen collections, it's necessary to address the most prominent reason why risks aren't taken in the first place: fear.

How will parents, the administration, and the community react to the materials the library makes available?

How it is possible to justify recommending this book to a teen?

Will the librarian get into trouble for aggressively weeding?

Essentially, what will the consequences be?

These are all valid questions and ones that librarians of all experience levels grapple with, despite their willingness to take risks. When selecting or deselecting an item, the librarian's name gets associated with that action, and it's possible it will be necessary to answer to someone because of it. That idea causes anxiety, which can sometimes influence actions. But it doesn't have to. By knowing what the risks are, preparing for any questions, and putting the needs of teens in the community first, the actual risk will seem much less frightening.

WHAT MAKES A TEEN COLLECTION RISKY?

Any time an item is added, displayed, or deleted, the collection's identity changes slightly. Add too much of one format, or delete too many books on one subject, and the identity becomes even more defined. This is a good thing! But it can be scary. Who are we trying to please? Ultimately the collection is for teens, but how often do librarians find themselves thinking about the reactions of fellow staff members, administrators, parents, and community members?

Potential controversy can inhibit decisions—if we let it. When Jamison Hedin started working as a librarian at Ludlow (Massachusetts) High School, she began to update the collection to enhance its appeal to teens. In the process, she drew some resistance from staff, but the feedback she got from students made it worth the risk. She told the authors,

> It's my second year in my position. Slowly, with limited budget resources, I'm working to update the print collection with fiction and high interest

nonfiction. The fiction collection I inherited had an average age of close to thirty years and was divided between classics and incredibly dated popular fiction from the 1970s and 1980s. I'm purchasing new YA titles, including works with street lit and GLBTQ themes—a first for this collection. I've also added the first graphic novels to the collection. There has been some resistance from faculty members, but the response from the students has been overwhelmingly positive.

THINKING ABOUT LEVELS OF COLLECTION DEVELOPMENT RISK

Jamison has taken several of the risks that will be addressed in this next section. Below are practices that could be considered risky. Some are high risk and others are minimal. Not every risk is right for every library; these are only examples of what others have done, some with varying degrees of success.

Content Risks

Action: buying materials with explicit sexual content, offensive language, or containing other controversial subjects

The risk: When it comes to the risks associated with collection development, fear of censure due to your decision to include specific materials usually ranks close to the top. These are the materials from which most challenges stem: profanity, depictions of homosexuality, or frank discussions of sex and sexuality. Holliston (Massachusetts) High School librarian mk Eagle told the authors about how she took on the risky challenge of incorporating these kinds of books into the collection during her first few months on the job:

> My predecessor kept a number of books—including many of the LGBTQ-themed books—in a back office where students had to ask to access them. My first book order contained a number of titles with queer themes, and I displayed them all proudly on our new books shelf.

Why it might be worth it: If it's risky for librarians to purchase and display the books, think about how risky it is for teens to check them out!

Librarians must set an example for teens by sending the message that their needs are being met before even having to ask. This is especially true when discussing sex-related topics (more on that and other risky subjects later in this chapter).

A little less risky: If your community or school is ultraconservative, test the waters with materials that are not quite so incendiary. Take a moment to think about why it's important to select certain items and

Profile of a Risk Taker: Beth Gallaway

I advocated for a YALSA-selected video games list in 1998. I made several inquiries about establishing a task force to investigate the possibility of the list, and as a result I was put on a task force to evaluate all selection lists. Learning about the process involved in change was eye-opening. I know now that talking to the right people and filling out the right paperwork are key!

I had success with YALSA establishing a Teen Gaming Discussion Group in 2007, which morphed into an interest group, and we put on a program and published a list of recommended games on a wiki.

Incidentally, my colleague John Scalzo of the Video Game Librarian fame created an award based on his blog—and the first awards were announced last year. I started my own e-mail discussion (with more than six hundred members) to talk about gaming in libraries, and I've gotten involved with the Office for Literacy and Outreach's efforts to tie *all* types of gaming to literacy for ages zero to eighteen.

Ultimately a selected list of video games for YALSA didn't work out, but the process was a learning experience. At the very least, I've raised the awareness in the profession about games as interactive digital storytelling.

what kind of benefit they can offer for teens. Inform administration about the reasons why these items are important for the collection. Then gradually begin to incorporate more of these books into the collection—and be prepared for challenges. Just remember: for every complaint you get, there are probably dozens of teens silently thanking the library for creating a collection that actually represents them.

Review Source Risks

Action: selecting items without professional reviews or recommended age ratings

The risk: The circumstances are anything but unique, and becoming more commonplace as the concept of a YA collection changes and grows. The teen librarian wants to purchase something for the library but can't find a review for it in any professional journal. It's even impossible to find an age rating from the publisher or vendor. What to do? Nontraditional items may be harder to justify because there is no one to back up the recommendation for purchase. What's worse, if the item were to be challenged, there is no expert besides the librarian selector to deem it acceptable for your collection.

Why it might be worth it: As the definition of a YA collection grows, it becomes more difficult to find reviews for everything. Does that mean the collection shouldn't include materials like manga, anime, and series paperbacks? Not at all. Rather as collection parameters grow, so must ideas of acceptable review sources. Why shouldn't a favorable customer review, a catchy cover the librarian knows will beg to be picked up by teens, or a request from a patron be counted? Popularity and demand are factors in any good selection policy. The sales rank in popular online stores, the number of copies ordered from publishers by vendors, or positive chatter from teens on social networking sites should all be factored into selection.

A little less risky: If a library needs an expert opinion, but can't find reviews to support a potential purchase, look to YALSA's selected lists. The titles on the Best Fiction for Young Adults lists will most likely have reviews, but books like the quirky nonfiction titles that have been nominated for the Quick Picks list might not. However, if a title is nominated for the Quick Picks list, that means it has been endorsed by at least one member of the committee, and probably field-tested with teens. Look into the policies, procedures, and processes of YALSA lists to justify selections. Aside from fiction and nonfiction, YALSA also has lists for graphic novels, audiobooks, and DVDs. Learn more about YALSA's lists at www.ala.org/yalsa/booklists.

If there are still collection areas that are not commonly covered by journals and award lists, remember that change is always possible. It wasn't long ago that graphic novels and games were rarely recognized; now they are included more often than not. It took graphic novel and gaming advocates to get these resources widely accepted. Be an advocate for change and be open to how a new genre or format might garner support.

Beth Gallaway, a private consultant who focuses on service to teens, has been a long-standing supporter of video games and their link to literacy. Beth took a risk by campaigning to create a YALSA selection list for video games. Her story demonstrates the risk in working for change, and how the results can sometimes be successful in different ways than initially expected. See p. 18 for Beth's story in her own words, from an interview with the authors.

The Risk of Adding Adult Materials

Action: placing materials in the teen section that were originally published for adults

The risk: Buying an item for the teen collection that was published with teens in mind is usually a safe bet. But including books that were published for adults next to teen books on the same shelf? Risky. By putting adult books in the teen collection, the library is implicitly recommending them for teens. Some of these titles may have extreme language, violence, and sexuality; placing them next to YA books may invite controversy.

Why it might be worth it: Teens aren't interested in what books they *should* be reading, only what they *want* to read. If librarians are successful in getting teens to read, then why should they be concerned with the collection designation? For example, street lit is immensely popular with teens. Though originally published for adults, many of the books are beloved favorites of urban teens. Megan Honig, young adult materials specialist with the New York Public Library, advocates for the inclusion of street lit into collections. In the 2008 *VOYA* article "Takin' It to the Street: Teens and Street Lit," she says, "Collecting street lit both supports teen reading and shows street-lit fans that they have a place in the library and in the community."[1] She later asserts that including street lit in the teen section can serve as "a way of inviting street-lit readers into the library's teen section and to facilitate their discovery of other genres that might be of interest." Any time it's possible to find a way to invite teens into their own space in the library and make them feel that they are heard and represented, that's success. Offering adult materials in the teen area is an effective method to achieve this, whether the adult books are controversial or simply marketed to adults, such as Jodi Picoult or Nicholas Sparks novels. In a 2009 *VOYA* article, "Crossing Over: Books from the Other Side," Candace Walton describes the ever-increasing blurred line between YA books and adult books. These crossover books share many of the same themes that appeal to teens, which means success for librarians: "Many young adult librarians embrace the crossover trend, believing chiefly that any book, whether written for adults or young adults, is a good thing if it gets teens reading and into the library."[2]

A little less risky: Maybe the budget simply can't accommodate the addition of adult books in the teen section. Public libraries can still provide access for these books by leaving markers in the teen area for how to find them in the adult section. Achieve this by creating print and online booklists for teens recommending certain adult titles; bringing cohesively themed books from the adult section for a display in the teen area; or posting signage in the teen area describing what else is available in the adult section and how to access it. As for school libraries, there are no adult sections to direct them to, unless you send them to the public library. Think about taking the leap for more mature materials, and let students be the guide as to what they enjoy and what they'd like to see in their school.

Is Leaving Dewey Behind Risky?

Action: eliminating Dewey decimal shelving and creating a bookstore atmosphere

The risk: Libraries and Dewey go hand-in-hand. It's what librarians know! It makes sense! For people familiar with the Dewey Decimal Classification system, finding a specific item is easy. And any time there is a major change in any organization, there is a prolonged adjustment period. Some might say, "If it ain't broke, don't fix it."

Why it might be worth it: Maybe it *is* broken. Librarians have little trouble navigating the shelves, but what about everyone else? Would they say they have an easier time finding books in the bookstore? What do teens— who, aside from required reading in school, probably just want to browse— think of Dewey? The Perry branch of the Maricopa County Library in Arizona opened in 2007, with nonfiction books shelved using the bookstore standard BISAC (Book Industry Standards and Communications) system.[3] Lauded for its simplicity and user-friendly approach, BISAC uses organizational concepts like those found at a bookstore, such as sections on gardening or cooking—a system that can be much less intimidating than numbers that can be eight digits long. The Maricopa Library made the switch after patron surveys showed that a majority of respondents indicated that they prefer to browse. If the BISAC system would help to create a more enjoyable browsing environment, why not do it? Since the Perry branch opened with BISAC shelving, libraries across the country have taken notice. Some have followed suit, while others have adopted a BISAC/Dewey hybrid. The key is to give teens every possible advantage for finding what they want— even what they don't know they want.

A little less risky: Another, less drastic way to achieve the easy accessibility of bookstore shelving, without abandoning Dewey altogether, is by shelving the same title in multiple locations. For example, copies of *A Child Called It* by Dave Pelzer could be shelved in both biographies and child abuse; Shakespeare titles could go in both plays and a required reading/classics section; and graphic novel companions to such fiction series as *Maximum Ride* by James Patterson and *Cirque du Freak* by Darren Shan could be shelved in both the graphic novels area and alongside their counterparts in the fiction section.

Risks in Meeting Individual Community Needs

Action: revamping a traditional library collection to meet the needs of the individual community

The risk: At first blush, revamping a teen collection doesn't seem risky at all. Librarians are reminded constantly about the need to stay relevant in this ever-changing time. But truly meeting the needs of some communities or school populations will mean different things and have different levels of risk. Maybe curriculum-based nonfiction is never going to circulate in a busy urban branch next to a school. Why keep it when part of the budget could be spent on more popular items like street lit? Perhaps the demand for video games forces cuts in other areas, such as nonfiction DVDs. Maybe books on CD sit dusty on the shelf. Taking the leap toward downloadable audio or Playaways might be the thing to do. Or even riskier—eliminate audiobooks altogether, if they're not circulating. Making major changes to any collection, especially if those changes mean less of what are described as beneficial or educational materials, means upsetting the status quo.

Why it might be worth it: Listening to what teens want and responding to their needs is the ultimate test of faith. Success means providing the best experience for the majority while still upholding the institution's mission. But take caution: while pleasing the target audience (teens), there might be others (parents, staff, and so on) who don't have the insider information available to librarians. Share surveys and statistics—numbers really do tell a story. Be prepared to defend decisions.

A little less risky: It's possible to reenergize the teen collection without venturing too far astray from the traditional collection. Carve out a portion of the budget so that the teen advisory board can purchase the materials of their choice; combine the reference and nonfiction section and begin circulating it all; interfile audiobooks with print fiction, and so on. Sometimes small efforts can result in a larger change in teen attitudes toward the library's offerings.

Risky Outsourcing

Action: outsourcing selection from the library to the vendor

The risk: The idea of putting your collection into the hands of vendors can be downright frightening. Vendors don't have a vested interest in the community, but they might have financial gain from favoring one publisher over another or one format over another. Additionally, outsourcing can lead people to wonder why librarian jobs are so important if someone three states away can do the work for less pay. Finally, to truly refine and perfect the outsourced selection could take years, an amount of time to which most libraries may not be willing to commit.

Why it might be worth it: Putting people—not materials—first is what will continue to make libraries relevant. By outsourcing collection development, librarians have more time for one-on-one interactions, outreach, searching for grant and funding opportunities, and so on. It also gives librarians time to focus on more specialized kinds of collection work, like weeding, updating collections, and analyzing circulation data to identify trends. When Phoenix Public Library began outsourcing their selection and turned a critical eye toward circulation reports, they found some surprising information. The truths they thought they knew weren't always the case, and they began a massive overhaul to beef up areas that were hot and weed those that got little attention.[4] In a time when budgets are shrinking, it's imperative to spend what is available on the most useful materials to teens. Outsourcing selection allows libraries to spend time researching trends and making personal connections to discover what it is teens really want.

A little less risky: Hand over the no-brainer selection, like best sellers, feature films, and top-selling music. Set up standing orders for well-known authors, series, and publishers. Ask the vendor to send lists at regular intervals that contain items reflecting the very detailed profile of your library provided to them. This allows the librarian to use selection time for work that requires more research and knowledge of your community.

The Risk in Personal Recommendations

Action: personally recommending books with risky topics to teens

The risk: Giving the right book to the right teen at the right time is the goal every YA librarian strives for, but sometimes the right book may invoke controversy. Parents may not be as pleased with the street-lit book as the teen who checked it out, and topics like sexuality can be seen as delicate too. "Each book we hand to a teen could result in a challenge," Kate Pickett, young adult librarian with the Johnson County Library in Kansas, revealed to the authors. When given a choice between recommending a book known to be perfect but potentially risky or an adequate book that won't make waves, what is the choice?

Why it might be worth it: They came to the librarian for a reason, right? Whether it's a first-time library user or one of the usual kids, asking an adult for advice is tough. Couple that with a risky topic and the situation becomes delicate. It's important to prove to the patron that she can trust the librarian's recommendations and that the librarian understands what it is she wants. Furthermore, it's important to recognize that what a teen is asking for may not be what she actually wants. "Books about dating" could mean "I need to know about sex, STDs, and contraception." The key is to listen, pick up on subtle hints, and offer up titles in an open manner. Equally important to earning teens' trust is for teens to earn the librarian's. Librarians must have faith that these are intelligent young adults who will read only what they themselves can handle. In a YALSA Blog post dated May 22, 2009, Teri Lesesne described a couple of challenges surrounding the novel *Wintergirls* by Laurie Halse Anderson, in which the main character suffers from anorexia.[5] She says, "This attempt to somehow protect teens from reading about any difficult issues and topics seems not always to be a matter of being overly protective. Rather it seems that we, as adults, are not giving teens sufficient credit for being intelligent beings, perfectly capable of reading about anorexia or sexual abuse or vampires or witchcraft without becoming anorexic (or becoming witches for that matter)." Librarians need to trust teens as much as we hope they'll trust us, and one very solid way to achieve this is through personalized book recommendations. Providing this kind of service will result in a loyal following.

A little less risky: Creating a display or booklist for a particular set of materials can highlight items that patrons may not know are available. In this instance, it's possible to light the path toward those risky books but not personally escort them down the path. It's less risky because with a display or booklist, it's the library that is making the recommendation; with a personal recommendation, the teen who receives the book will remember the librarian who gave it to him. But a bigger risk may mean greater returns—the personal recommendation will establish a personal connection where the display or booklist won't. Why not do both?

Weeding Can Be Risky

Action: aggressively weeding the collection

The risk: Weeding the collection can provoke outcries from staff and public alike. Aside from throwing out the obvious—outdated information and low-circulating materials—often weeding becomes a series of judgment calls. Using personal judgment rather than following a strict set of rules is really the riskiest practice, because decisions may be harder to defend. When it comes to a teen collection, because of the ever-changing nature of the content in which teens are interested, it's important to be even more aggressive than in areas suited toward other age groups.

Why it might be worth it: Judgment is really crucial here, because the librarian knows the collection and the community best. A book may have a spectacular story or contain key information for a student's report. However, no teen will pick those up if the cover features teens from ten years ago sporting fashions no longer remembered. Even fonts and graphics have a way of looking dated and teens will most definitely pick up on this. The reward for doing away with the old? More shelf space to create a browsing collection and higher interest as a whole. It also sends teens an important message: "We recognize you have taste standards and we'll do our best to respect that." When in doubt, throw it out—if something is really good, there'll be an updated cover for it. If the library can't afford the new reprint, create a wish list of items and shop it around to teachers, staff, parents, Friends, and so forth.

A little less risky: Still weed, but take some of the items that seem like judgment calls, ones that cause apprehension, to the next teen advisory board meeting. Explain the weeding policy to them and ask for the teens' opinions. Then use their expert opinions to back you when someone questions the decision.

Going Digital Is Risky Business

Action: eliminating books in favor of an entirely digital collection

The risk: Books = libraries = books. Period. To remove the books would cause an uproar.

Why it might be worth it: Think about what the patrons' needs are. Do they use the facility just for research? How would redirecting the book budget into online resources and technology help research needs? Cushing Academy in Ashburnham, Massachusetts, went all digital for their 2009–2010 school year.[6] In redesigning the library to feature laptop-friendly carrels and huge flat-screen TVs projecting Internet data, they haven't given up entirely on books—just the printed format. They loan Sony Readers that can hold hundreds of books at a time. Yes, many people (including librarians) think it's crazy. Yet by focusing on the needs of patrons and the organization's mission, it's possible to find that it actually makes sense.

A little less risky: Maybe going completely digital doesn't make sense because it's not what's best for your patrons or budget. But it's still possible to use the principle of this risk—disregarding format in favor of content—and it may be prime for some smaller risks. Maybe it makes sense to eliminate curriculum-related nonfiction in favor of databases, highlighted access to authoritative websites, or real-time online homework help services. Where can the budget be spent most wisely while serving the most teens possible?

POLICIES

While developing a teen collection is always a risky business, not all risks are created equal. Here is where the calculated risk comes in: by creating a solid collection development policy that will cover most, if not all, situations. Whether the details of teen collections are covered in the library's broader policy or if you have a policy specific to teen services, it is imperative that the language be encompassing, flexible, and allow for taking risks.

A good policy should cover the philosophy behind selection and should allow for future technologies to be implemented seamlessly. Consider potential hurdles that may be faced in taking risks with the collection and speak to them in the policy. Make sure to cover the following:

> **Age.** Who is this collection meant for? Who is the primary community? Also address how items that are appropriate for eighteen-year-olds may not be suitable for twelve-year-olds, and so forth.

> **Genres and formats.** What will one find in the teen collection? What won't they find?

> **Selection criteria and resources.** What will be considered when making selections and what types of resources will be consulted in order to determine what materials are added?

Weeding guidelines. This should include the philosophy of weeding along with general information about how often weeding needs to take place.

The procedure to respond to patron challenges or inquiries.

Now that the basics are covered in the policy, go back through it to see how flexible it is in terms of risk taking. If a move is made from DVDs to downloadable video, will it still work? If selections are made using teen reviews on Goodreads or *Teen Vogue*'s book forum, can the purchase still be justified?

The next step is to make the collection development policy available online. Some libraries might see this as a risk but it sends a message that says, "We're not trying to hide anything. If you take the time to read this, we'll take the time to follow it." See p. 29 for examples of teen-specific policies.

Say you've crafted a policy that allows risks. It's published. Does the staff buy into it? While it seems natural that all staff members would support a policy that encourages access and discourages censorship, it's still a good idea to bring any changes to light and get everyone on board. Maybe someone doesn't understand why the library is now buying street lit for the teen section, or why the library stopped buying curriculum-related nonfiction. This is the chance to get practice in defending risky decisions and to garner support for the changes. Chances are these are the folks that will most often communicate directly with patrons, so it's vital that they understand and support the new policy.

Finally, perhaps the biggest risk of all could be not having a collection development policy. Through the policy, it's possible to create a safety net for all the risks taken via collections; the policy is definitely a sound investment. Yet some believe that by not having a policy at all, it can give the library the freedom to select without inhibition. How's that for the ultimate risk?

APPROACHING RISKY TOPICS

With a solid collection development policy and a clear mission, there should be few subjects that are off limits in the teen collection. However,

Teen Collection
Development Policies

When looking for examples of collection development policies for teen library collections, try these:

Haverhill Public Library in Haverhill, Massachusetts.
www.haverhillpl.org/About/policies/teenmaterials.html.
Has a separate collection policy for teen materials and is referenced in the general policy

J. W. Mitchell High School in New Port Richey, Florida.
http://mitchellonline.pasco.k12.fl.us/~media/Media/Academic_Media_files/ MHS%20Collection%20Development%20Policy.pdf.
Covers general collection points as well as those specific to the school environment

Monterey Public Library in Monterey, California.
www.monterey.org/library/cdp/cdp13.html.
Offers specific teen information within the context of the whole library's policy

San Francisco Public Library in San Francisco, California.
http://sfpl.org/index.php?pg=2000011101.
The teen section of the overall policy is very specific in terms of what the collection offers for teens.

Whitefish High School Library in Whitefish, Montana.
http://wfps.k12.mt.us/Teachers/KohnstammD/Collection%20Dev%27t%20 Policy%20for%20Web.htm.
Describes their community and user groups both within and beyond the student body

it's always best to anticipate which topics will likely be most controversial, allowing staff to recognize the risks in adding them to the collection. According to ALA's Office of Intellectual Freedom, sex, profanity, and racism continue to top the list of reasons why books are challenged.[7] "The big three" should be acknowledged in the selection process, if only to make sure the library can justify the purchase and ensure that its policy defends the selection of materials that discuss those topics. It's also important to recognize what a balanced collection means. For example, if a book includes homosexuality, many believe the appropriate balance to that is offering Christian-themed books. Actually, the balance to homosexual themes is the portrayal of a heterosexual lifestyle. Books featuring Christianity can be balanced with those of other faiths, information about teens engaging in sexual activity can be balanced with information about abstinence, and so forth.

Note how your community may react to a particular subject area. In a 2009 YALSA Blog post, Jen Waters wrote about a delicate situation at her library.[8] She purchased *The Book of Bunny Suicides* for her library, and her coworker—who recently lost her daughter to suicide—objected. Jen didn't pull the book, but was concerned about responding sensitively to her coworker. Kate Pickett recently found herself in a similar situation at a middle school where she planned to booktalk a book about suicide. "I was told that it may not be a good idea to booktalk the book as the school had experienced a suicide only the year before. I talked about the book anyway and several students told me they were interested in reading it. However, now thinking back on it, if there were heat to be caught in this situation, not only would it fall on me but on the teacher that invited me to the school. Sometimes we are taking risks with more than just ourselves." Jen's and Kate's stories illuminate how extenuating circumstances can change the risk factor. Despite the potential pain the inclusion of these books might cause, both librarians chose to take the risk in hopes of providing the best service to teens, which is commendable.

Graphic novels represent another risky area. Patrons may raise little or no objection to a sex scene in a traditional YA novel, while a graphic novel's illustration of the same scene could illicit furious complaints. But just as all descriptions in prose are different, so are all graphic illustrations. Treat each book individually. If you're researching a controversial item to add to your collection and don't have access to the item, then look for reviews, ratings, or sample pages online to gauge the content for yourself. Look to demand for the item and find the most appropriate collection to place it in.

Finally, the most important aspect to think about in terms of risky topics is one's own perceptions versus reality. Sometimes librarians expect certain materials to cause a fervor when they blow over quite quickly. In 2005, the book *Rainbow Party* by Paul Ruditis drew intense speculation. The story revolves around an upcoming high school party in which all the attendees will engage in oral sex (the "rainbow" comes from each girl wearing a different color lipstick), and the characters who will be attending. Each character has a reason to go to the party, and a reason for being petrified of it. In the end, the party doesn't happen—kind of like the built-up anxiety librarians and booksellers felt about the book. Neither Borders nor Barnes and Noble carried the book in stores (but both made it available online). Many libraries didn't buy it. And despite the media hype around it, the book didn't sell. Many agreed that the topic was interesting but the story itself wasn't well-written.[9] Contrary to predictions, teens didn't clamor for it or pass it on to each other, pages dog-eared. On the other hand, take a book like John Green's *Looking for Alaska*, the 2006 Michael L. Printz winner. No one expected it to show up year after year on ALA's frequently banned books lists. The language can be coarse and there is sexual content, but most important the story is compelling— which makes teens pass it on to each other after reading. The moral of the story? It's good to be aware of the buzz going on with a book, but it's even better to investigate.

In this respect, Jamison Hedin says,

> I'm realizing more and more that what constitutes a risk for one professional in one working environment and community culture may not be a risk at all for someone else, working somewhere else. For me, recommending *Tweak* for the summer reading list was a big risk, and it's been somewhat controversial. I would imagine that elsewhere, it would not be a risk at all. Risk is relative. As professionals, I think it's important to think about risks in context and to celebrate them—whether small or large.

Each librarian is the best judge for community temperament. If patrons or fellow staff members mention that a book will generate controversy, request an advance readers' copy from the publisher and read it. Know that there is a certain blindness going into selection. No one can predict which books will be classic favorites and which will be tossed aside. But ultimately, it's best to let your teen patrons do the tossing.

HOW RISKY COLLECTIONS SUPPORT TEENS

We've identified the risks in collection development, created a policy and encouraged staff buy-in. Now we come full circle to the reason for creating these collections in the first place: to provide the best experience possible for teens. As noted in chapter 1, the Search Institute's Forty Developmental Assets for Adolescents (ages twelve to eighteen) are "40 common sense, positive experiences and qualities that help influence choices young people make and help them become caring, responsible adults." [10] The list describes experiences teens have and qualities they learn at home, school, and in their community. Not every one includes the work done in libraries but many of them do. For a look at all forty of the developmental assets, see appendix D; below are the five that will thrive with positive-risk collection development.

Caring School Climate. School provides a caring, encouraging environment. School libraries can provide the kinds of materials and formats that encourage students to thrive.

Community Values Youth. A young person perceives that adults in the community value youth. Youth will feel valued if the kinds of materials they like are available for them. This may include some riskier formats, genres, and topics.

Reading for Pleasure. A young person reads for pleasure three or more hours per week. When teens are given carte blanche to read whatever they want, including online reading and audiobooks, they are more likely to continue to do so.

Youth as Resources. Young people are given useful roles in the community. Want to offer teens exactly what they want so they'll feel valued? Want to encourage reading for pleasure? Ask them what they like to read, and really listen to the answers.

Personal Power. A young person feels she has control over "things that happen to me." Teens go through many firsts in adolescence. By providing top-notch information about whatever new experiences they're having, librarians send a message that teens can control their lives through knowledge.

GOING OUT INTO THE COMMUNITY

The last step in providing risky collections to support teens is informing the community about the importance of such materials. This doesn't mean holding a town hall meeting, but it does mean being prepared to discuss specific decisions and risk as a whole. Without risk, libraries can fall prey to:

Self-censorship. Has there ever been something you chose not to purchase for a collection? How did it feel after the decision was made? Later, did you wish that it had been purchased? What about something you purchased that caused problems? Did it change selection practices afterwards?

Stagnancy. If you don't push boundaries to bring new items into the collection, kids will get bored. Think of what your library meant twenty years ago and what it is now. Someone had to take a risk to be the first to bring movies, music, graphic novels, and video games into libraries. Where would we be without these pioneers?

Irrelevance. If we don't stay current, then teens won't care.

Erin Downey Howerton says, "If we're not speaking up in order to provide patrons with what they want and need, then we're not doing our jobs right—period. Libraries are combination intellectual factories/warehouses and risk is inherent in our work." The key for risky collections is laying a foundation that allows for risk and building a strong collection development policy as well as a supportive team of library staffers. Combine that with a real working knowledge of what teens in the community want, and the library will be set.

NOTES

1. Megan Honig, "Takin' It to the Street: Teens and Street Lit," *Voice of Youth Advocates* 31, no. 3: 207–11.

2. Candace Walton, "Crossing Over: Books from the Other Side," *Voice of Youth Advocates* 32, no. 5 (December 2009): 388–91.

3. Barbara Fister, "The Dewey Dilemma," *Library Journal*, October 1, 2009, www.libraryjournal.com/article/CA6698264.html.

4. Barbara Hoffert, "Who's Selecting Now?" *Library Journal*, September 1, 2007, www.libraryjournal.com/article/CA6471081.html.

5. Teri Lesesne, "Dangerous Minds," YALSA Blog, http://yalsa.ala.org/blog/2009/05/22/dangerous-minds.

6. David Abel, "Welcome to the Library. Say Goodbye to the Books," Boston.com, September 4, 2009, www.boston.com/news/local/massachusetts/articles/2009/09/04/a_library_without_the_books.

7. Robert P. Doyle, "Books Challenged & Banned 2008–2009," www.ala.org/ala/issuesadvocacy/banned/bannedbooksweek/ideasandresources/free_downloads/2009banned.pdf.

8. Jen Waters, "*The Book of Bunny Suicides*," YALSA Blog, http://yalsa.ala.org/blog/2009/09/26/the-book-of-bunny-suicides.

9. Carol Memmott, "Controversy Colors Teen Book," *USA Today*, May 22, 2005, www.usatoday.com/life/books/news/2005-05-22-rainbow-usat_x.htm.

10. The Search Institute, "Developmental Assets Tools," www.search-institute.org/assets.

3

Risk-Worthy Collections
What Authors Have to Say

Chapter 2 described the kinds of risky challenges librarians face when creating collections for teens. These collections could contain everything from books published for young adults to graphic novels, feature films, popular music, e-books, street lit, and more. Risks surface around a material's content, format, and availability. But what do authors think about risk when it comes to writing their books, the teens who read them, and the librarians who put them on their shelves (or not, as the case may be)?

In this chapter, four amazing, risk-taking authors speak about the risks they take when writing about touchy topics such as suicide, sex, abuse, and LGBTQ issues. But each one also contemplates the risks librarians take when purchasing their works for library collections. The authors were interviewed in November and December of 2009.

ELLEN HOPKINS

Q. Which of your books do you think required the biggest risks?
A. *Identical* and *Tricks*

Q. Why were those titles so risky?
A. *Identical* looks at childhood sexual abuse . . . incest. Even the word
       is hard to say. Actually looking at what that means is not something

people want to do (but it's something we *must* do). *Tricks* is about teen prostitution. There is sex in the book (it's prostitution!!), and it isn't pretty sex. Both books are honest, raw, and necessary.

Q. What did your editor say?

A. My editor, Emma Dryden, supports me totally. In fact, I sort of waited to see if she'd ask me to pull back a little, waiting to defend the more difficult scenes. She never did, and to give Simon and Schuster credit, neither did they.

Q. What did reviews say?

A. *Identical* got two starred reviews. *Tricks*, though termed "graphic," has received excellent reviews. Both books have been called things like "disturbing" or "not for the faint of heart," but reviewers, too, seem to understand that the subject matter is important. Also, because my books are so character-driven, readers become invested in the characters, which propels them through the harder passages.

Q. What did teens say?

A. I've probably heard from three or four who told me they had to put the books down. But I've heard from thousands more who thanked me for them. Victims of incest have thanked me for not closing that bedroom door and letting readers assume what's going on. Because the assumption might be it didn't really happen, or what happened wasn't that bad. And even teens whose lives have never been touched by anything remotely like this appreciate being considered mature and sophisticated enough to handle this subject matter. In high school, I didn't have good YA to read, so I went straight to adult stuff including V. C. Andrews, Jean Auel, Jacqueline Suzanne, and even Erica Jong.

Q. What did librarians say?

A. There are still some librarians who want to be gatekeepers and refuse to understand that today's teens are, indeed, sophisticated enough to handle this kind of material. However, they are a (literally and figuratively) dying breed. Most librarians (and I talk to a lot of them, believe me) understand that kids today are not only reading about addiction, abuse, thoughts of suicide, etc., but living those things. Librarians, for the most part, respect the kids they see and know which ones need most to read about kids like themselves, so they know they're not alone. When the inevitable challenges come, they face them head on. I love librarians!

Q. Will you take this type of risk again?

A. Of course! I don't write to please the gatekeepers. I write important books that speak to today's teens (and older). I don't write for the money, or to be gratuitous. I write to touch lives.

Q. What would you like to say to librarians who might be afraid to put risky books like yours on their shelves?

A. It would be nice to give kids nice, scrubbed childhoods. Unfortunately, life rarely offers them that. Better to give them the tools they need to make the right choices. As I wrote in my poem "Manifesto," "Ignorance is no armor." But knowledge is a great weapon. We need to break stereotypes, to change statistics like "one in four young women and one in seven young men will be raped or sexually abused before they turn twenty-one." We do that by dragging these issues out into the light of day. Certainly, they aren't new. But historically, we closed our eyes to them, choosing instead to be victimized by them. Today, with knowledge as our weapon, we have to say, "No more."

BARRY LYGA

Q. Which of your books do you think required the biggest risks?

A. I know what you're expecting here, but the honest answer is that each book required big risks. They were just different kinds of risks. That first book was my first foray into YA, which felt very risky at the time. *Hero-Type* was a risk because I knew people would be expecting something more like *Boy Toy*. *Goth Girl Rising* was a *huge* risk because I was writing as a girl, when I had built my reputation as a boy writer. Even *Wolverine* was a risk because I didn't know if people would respond to me writing something sort of fun and goofy.

But, yeah, *Boy Toy* had risks all its own, and that's the book most people automatically think of.

Q. Why was that title so risky?

A. For *Boy Toy*, the big thing, of course, was the sex. It wasn't just the mere fact of the sex—it was that the sex took place between a twelve-year-old boy and a twenty-four-year-old woman and for most of the book, the perspective on the sex was that it was good. Josh enjoyed having sex with Eve. Loved every minute of it. It's not until the end of the book that he acknowledges that it was wrong, that he'd been abused, so for most of the book, I'm depicting an immoral, illegal relationship, but the main character is saying, "And it's *great!*"

People are touchy enough about sex in books for teens to begin with. When you write about child abuse and have a character say it's all right (even if that character is proven wrong by story's end), people really get twisted into knots.

The funny thing about that book, though . . . I challenge people to re-read it and pay particular attention to the sex scenes. They're not *nearly* as explicit or graphic as people tend to think they are. Most of the "action" happens between the lines and in the reader's imagination.

Q. What did your editor say?

A. I blush to say it, but she was extremely complimentary and heaped all kinds of praise upon it. She also said it was too long and that I needed to cut two hundred pages. (That first draft was much longer.) I think I ended up cutting north of a hundred pages, and we came to a compromise length that made us both happy.

Q. What did reviews say?

A. Again, blushing, but the reviews were uniformly, overwhelmingly positive and effusive. I think there was one that I remember that seemed to hedge a little bit, but I know that for a while there, it seemed like every day brought a new, amazing review. It was quite an experience. *Boy Toy* is, without a doubt, my best-reviewed book.

Q. What did teens say?

A. I have yet to hear from a teen who didn't like it. But more important than that are the teens I've heard from who really got something out of the book, who came to understand an abused friend or loved one. I heard from some kids who'd been abused themselves who really appreciated someone writing down what they felt.

Q. What did librarians say?

A. As with reviewers, it was almost uniformly positive and encouraging. The sad part, though, is the librarians who said they loved the book, but they didn't feel they could recommend it to kids.

Q. Will you take this type of risk again?

A. God, yes. I take risks with every book I write. I don't see the point in writing books if you're not going to take risks. The only way to grow and improve as a writer is to challenge yourself, and you can't do that if you're writing the same book over and over again, afraid to branch out, afraid to try new things.

Q. What would you like to say to librarians that might be afraid to put risky books like yours on their shelves?

A. This is difficult to answer because—obviously—there's an element to this that transcends mere freedom-to-read. Which is to say, people's jobs could be at stake. If someone puts a risky book on the shelf and it causes a confrontation, this person could end up fired. Or in a tussle that has long-lasting ramifications personally, professionally, health-wise, etc. So I would never say, "Put my risky books on your shelves or you are a bad person!" That's not my place.

What I would say is this: Information and ideas are important. Your job is to disseminate that information. The forces arrayed against you, the people who *don't* want that information to be disseminated, are working against not just you, not just my book, but against every person who needs information and cannot find it.

The truly disturbing facet of all this is the way that the forces against information hardly have to lift a finger these days. One librarian e-mailed to tell me that she loved *Boy Toy* so much that she read it three times . . . and then said, "But I can't put it on my shelf. I might get in trouble." She "might" get in trouble. Might. Based on nothing more than the perception and the possibility, she did not put the book on the shelf, and the "bad guys" won. They won without firing a shot. They won without a struggle. They won without even knowing that there was a fight! Because there was no fight. Just a unilateral surrender before the fact.

If you think there "might" be a problem with a book and it's a problem with fallout you personally are not willing to handle, then don't just give up. Ask around. Talk to a supervisor. Make sure there's going to be a problem. Find out if there's a way around the problem. If you're going to surrender, do it because you made a good faith effort. Do it because of an actual problem or issue, not one you think might, maybe, someday exist.

Make no mistake: You are a crucial player in a battle against the reactionary tides of ignorance. Your decision must be whether or not you will participate in the battle. I'm not here to tell you what your decision should be. I just want you to know what the stakes are before you make up your mind.

LAUREN MYRACLE

Q. Which of your books do you think required the biggest risks?

A. I didn't think in terms of "risks" when I wrote my first novel, *Kissing Kate*, but it turns out that girls kissing girls is indeed a risky subject. Girls and sexuality, period (and girls' periods!) are also risky, it turns out, and the treatment of those subjects in the Internet Girls series, as well as the Winnie Years series, has drawn lots of less-than-enthusiastic response.

Q. Why were those titles so risky?

A. I think some adults are uncomfortable with sexuality, especially when it comes to tweens and teens, and especially when it comes to girls. It's the whole "protect our innocent darlings" mentality, and also, I suspect, a totally understandable desire to keep kids in the safe bubble of childhood until they're forty.

Q. What did your editor say?

A. Susan, who worked with me on the Internet Girls series, said, "People think girls don't talk about sex. Guess what? They do. I love how honestly you portray the issues girls struggle with these days. Go for it."

Julie, who worked with me on the Winnie Years series, said, "Love it. Wish I'd had a guide to girlhood like this when I was twelve. People are going to have problems with the tampon scene, but they'll just have to deal with it."

Q. What did reviews say?

A. Oh, a mix. Some commented negatively on what they perceived as unnecessary vulgarity and sexual explicitness; others praised the same qualities, but used adjectives like "brave," "authentic," and "real."

Q. What did teens say?

A. Also a mix! Ha. But with a much different ratio of negative to positive comments. I'd say 90 percent of the e-mails I get about the Internet Girls series are super enthusiastic, with the girls saying things like, "I can't believe you're a grown-up. Seriously. How do you know how we think?" But there are also girls who write and say, "I loved the books, but I don't understand why you used bad language. The books would have been just as good without that."

As for the Winnie Years books, however, adults are the only ones who have a problem with the chapters dealing with bras, menstruation, and the general bizarro land of puberty. The girls who write me? They just say "thanks," and that they wish they had a friend like Winnie in real life.

Q. What did librarians say?

A. A sampling:

"Oh, the girls love your books. We can't keep them on the shelves!"

"I applaud you for what you do, but I have to keep your titles hidden on the counter. I give them only to girls if I know their parents won't cause a fuss."

"Can you come speak to our high school students? Great! But please don't mention *ttyl* or those other instant messaging books."

"The kids loved your visit. They absolutely adore Winnie! But between you and me, I am *so* glad you didn't read the tampon scene. I was so afraid you might!"

Q. **Will you take this type of risk again?**

A. Forever and ever, amen. Why? Because the point of writing, for me, is to try my best to offer a glimpse of the world that's true, so that readers can take those ideas in, process them in a safe and private way, and decide for themselves what they think.

Q. **What would you like to say to librarians that might be afraid to put risky books like yours on their shelves?**

A. I'd paraphrase the brilliant David Levithan, who said something like this in response to a librarian who expressed fear of losing her job if she put books like *ttyl* on her shelves: "What's the point of having your job if you're not doing your job? A librarian's job is to serve *all* students, and a librarian who only puts 'safe' books on the shelves is failing to do that."

I'd also tell them to be brave, take a stand, and make considered decisions about what books they're willing to fight for. And, of course, have your rationales ready. And after they did put risky books on their shelves? I'd high-five them and say, "Thanks, librarian-person! You rock!!!!!!"

ALEX SANCHEZ

Q. **Which of your books do you think required the biggest risks?**

A. Riskiest was my first novel, *Rainbow Boys*. Next riskiest was my most recent novel, *Bait*.

Q. **Why were those titles so risky?**

A. The risk of rejection when starting out as a writer is huge. Since before *Rainbow Boys* I'd never been published, it was a risk to spend hours creating something that no one would want to read. The manuscript was the first time I'd ever been truly honest in my writing. I was only able to take that risk with the encouragement of friends. With *Bait*, the biggest risk was in writing about something as personal and painful as sexual abuse. It's a risk to be vulnerable to others. But there can be no reward without risk. For me, the reward in writing is to hear when readers connect.

Q. **What did your editor say?**

A. For *Rainbow Boys*, he saw the book as groundbreaking. Previously, a handful of other YA novels with teen gay characters portrayed them as isolated and struggling with their sexuality. The risky newness here was portraying gay teens as natural, normal kids for whom the problem wasn't being gay but rather a society that didn't want to accept them. The good news was the love, friendship, and connection they were able to find with each other. For *Bait*, he was excited by the portrayal of a complex character who was neither exclusively victim nor victimizer, challenging the usual either/or views of people.

Q. **What did reviews say?**

A. For *Rainbow Boys*, the most memorable review was from a librarian who said, "have the courage to make it available . . . it can open eyes and change lives." For *Bait*, "Unlike most recent fiction that addresses sexual abuse, this story focuses not on the telling of secrets, but on making sense of the experience and building a healthy foundation for moving forward . . . High interest and accessible, this coming-of-age story belongs in every collection."

Q. **What did teens say?**

A. What's been so amazing with the Rainbow trilogy has been the thousands of e-mails from teens who say how the books inspired them to take new steps in their lives: to accept themselves, to come out, to be more accepting of others, or to start a gay-straight alliance at their school. With *Bait*, it's been tremendously moving to hear from boys and girls who have been abused or know someone who has and how the book helps them to heal.

Q. **What did librarians say?**

A. The consensus from librarians about the Rainbow books seems to be how difficult it is to keep enough copies in circulation. Yay! With *Bait*, many are thrilled to have a book that addresses tough emotional issues among boys. They want more books about boys that focus on issues other than sports and competition.

Q. **Will you take this type of risk again?**

A. I have to. Risk is what keeps me writing. Every manuscript has had its own risks. With *So Hard to Say*, the risk was to write from a female protagonist's point of view. With *Getting It*, the risk was to portray a homophobic straight teenage boy becoming friends with an outspokenly gay boy. With *The God Box*, it was to tackle conflicts of spirituality and sexuality. Risk is what keeps the writing fresh and passionate for me and hopefully for the reader, too.

Q. **What would you like to say to librarians that might be afraid to put risky books like yours on their shelves?**

A. I understand that librarians may find themselves on the frontlines of challenges. And I'm impressed by the willingness of so many who are willing to risk those challenges because of their passion to present a diversity of voices, librarians who went into the field because of their desire to spread knowledge, and who recognize how books can inspire and empower young people. I'd encourage fearful librarians to reach out and seek support from those who have dealt with their fears about risky books and who have reaped the rewards of taking risks. You're my heroes!

Librarians are authors' heroes? Certainly the feeling is mutual! From these interviews, it's easy to see that we're all on the same page, so to speak, when it comes to getting teens the information they need in order to become healthy, happy, self-sufficient, world-wise adults.

4

Risks in Programming
A Necessity

Programming for teens in libraries is a great way to tie all aspects of teen librarianship into one (or two, or three, or more) amazing event. It encompasses nearly all the work teen librarians do: talking with teens, building collections, mobilizing staff expertise, planning, advertising, and more.

But what makes teen programming risky? What does risky teen programming look like in libraries? It depends on how the librarian mixes together different elements of programming. A successful formula for teen programming in any library might look like this:

teens + library resources + you = fabulous library program

Risk can enter the scene at any point in the equation.

**risky teens + risky library resources + (most of all) risky you! =
fabulous risky library program**

RISKY PROGRAMMING IN THE KNOW

Before beginning to think about taking risks in programs, however, keep the following advice in mind:

Know the audience. Talking regularly to the teens in your library, neighborhood schools, and the community makes it possible to correctly gauge just how much risk to take. Talking with teens should provide a hint as to what kind of audience a program will draw. Remember, a risky program with no audience isn't much of a success. Be sure that the risk taken is something teens will appreciate and support by attending. A successful program makes it possible to brag to the director and community members. It will also be possible to highlight that taking a risk was well worth it.

Know the community. Be honest: hosting a graffiti art dance party in a conservative community is not the best first programming risk to take. Rather, take what's known about the community and think deeply and carefully about how to turn teens' amazing, groundbreaking ideas into something that won't send the rest of the community or library staff, into an uproar.

Know the library administration. The administration is the best supporter for teen programming. Be sure to keep them in the loop with any teen programming—risky or not—planned for the library. After the program, let administrators know about the success of the risky program. Highlight why the risk was worth it and how taking it added to the success of the program.

Acknowledge limits. Recognize that everyone has different comfort levels. It's okay to be uncomfortable hosting a street-lit book discussion group with teens. Maybe someone else on staff isn't! Moreover, if a program faces strong opposition from the library director, be honest with the teens at the library about its chances. Or if teens are asking for programming that challenges staff comfort levels, try to figure out how to accommodate teen ideas by reimagining the program into something that integrates a piece of the original idea, but is not quite as risky. Developing something that includes a less-risky aspect of a program can demonstrate to colleagues what's possible, create a positive buzz, and make it possible to take more risks next time around. Never be afraid to take baby steps to build future support for bigger, more important risks.

FAST OR SLOW MOVEMENT IN TAKING PROGRAMMING RISKS

The first step in figuring out what's possible in teen library programming is to use the framework laid out in the previous section. It will be helpful in deciding how risky to actually be. And it's possible to also use the structure that follows to figure out how quickly to move forward with risky teen programming.

Take Baby Steps When:

- The library has never hosted teen programs before. Ever. But the library has given the teen librarian the go-ahead to launch teen programming.
- The library is in a more conservative area; community values might not equate to what teens in the library are requesting.
- The director or administrator is timid when it comes to having teens in the library or hosting events specifically for them. No one in the library has ever heard of a teen advisory board, and they're even afraid to ask what it is and what it can accomplish!

How to be risky: Proceed with caution. In a situation in which teen programming is an entirely new initiative, everything is risky and baby steps are key. The secret to success is knowing what the administrator will support and what will be harder to sell. Remember, the best path may be the careful one that slowly builds into a strong, dynamic teen program that is stable and supports all of the needs of the teens in the community. Be sure to communicate the reasons for baby steps with teens. Once they understand the library process, they'll be better informed on how to advocate for both themselves and the library.

Take Bigger Steps When:

- The community may not be the dictionary definition of progressive, but it's clear that people are open to new ideas—especially those that support teen development. Adults who frequent the library understand that teens need to be teens, so complaints about behavior are few and far between, even during busier hours.

- The library has a history of programs for teens, and might even have a space for teens, and a collection. The director requires reports on all teen activities that the library sponsors. The teen librarian has worked in the library for several months, and has had the opportunity to lead teen programs—maybe even a teen advisory board—from time to time.

How to be risky: Move quickly and be sure to keep library staff and the community in the loop on all teen programming. Be sure to let community members know when a teen program is happening so they can plan their own schedules accordingly (i.e., to be at the library on that day, or not). Audience-building is also key: focus on hosting teen programs once per week on the same day. Creating a regular schedule lets teens and their parents know to come to the library on that specific day of the week for awesome programs. Other patrons will learn not to come on those days of the week to avoid any additional noise, rowdiness, enthusiasm, and so forth on the part of the teens that the program may illicit.

Being in this situation provides leeway for trying new ideas and pushing the boundaries of teens' expectations for programming. Ask teens to come up with some out-of-the-box ideas and talk with administrators and community members about those ideas. Administrators and community members might not be open at first, but the more the topic is discussed, the more they'll listen. Risks in programming when working at this level may be related to program content, such as tackling issues like teen pregnancy or risqué books. Or perhaps this is the perfect time to tackle a new format, such as gaming.

Take a Leap Forward When:

- The library has a teen area, if not a teen center. Programs occur on a daily basis, and there are several staff members dedicated to teens.
- There is a great collection, great administrative and community support, and a history of groundbreaking teen programs.
- The director is excited to hear reports about teen services, and teen services are on equal footing with the adult and children's departments.
- The community is used to big teen programs at the library, and

there is a dedicated teen audience for many, if not most, of the programs, which happen daily.

- There is a dedicated teen advisory board that meets weekly to discuss plans for the library, and the teen librarian knows the right pathways to execute those plans.

How to be risky: Go for it. There is support from both administration and the community. There are funds from grants or the development office, and it's obviously time to roll. The director is open to any idea that gets teens through the doors of the library, or using the library's services virtually, and he is willing to help the teen librarian find the time and the funds to make it happen.

This is perhaps a fairly progressive community, with lots of support from parents, schools, community-based organizations, and the grass-roots relationships built with the teens who frequent the library. The library and librarians likely achieved this strong support with backing from several administrators, so it's important to keep supervisors and the director in the loop on all program planning and accomplishments. That support needs to continue when risks in programming start happening.

Risks in programming may come when tackling controversial issues, new program formats, or inviting new audiences into the library. Remember: be fearless! There's a track record, and administrative support often follows that record.

Once it's determined how fast or slow to go with risk taking in programming, teen librarians will be better qualified to gauge what types of risks to take.

RISKS IN DEVELOPING THE AUDIENCE

Many libraries see a core audience of teen visitors every day. They come to programs, hang out at the desk with the librarian, and ask for reading recommendations.

But what about the teens who don't come into the library yet or the teens who drop in to check out books and make their exit before anyone can pitch a program to them? What are their needs? What about teens in the community who are out of school and need to earn their GED? Is there a Gay-Straight Alliance (GSA) in the neighborhood high school or middle school? Are there homeless teens who come to the library? Are there teens with special needs in the community? Chances are one of these groups —and likely most—is part of the library's community, and it's up to the teen librarian to figure out where they are and how to get them into the library with fun, effective, and interesting programs.

Start by going where the teens are. If a teen GSA meets at the high school, then the teen librarian could attend one or more meetings to introduce himself, find out what types of programs the teens in the group would like to have at the library, and maybe even plan a library program as a part of the meeting agenda. Visit the local homeless shelter and talk with teens there, or visit the adult basic education program where teens might be taking classes to successfully complete a GED.

Of course, these scenarios require the teen librarian to spend time outside the library building, which some administrators and colleagues might consider inappropriate. So going outside could be risky. But if in the long run, leaving the building brings teens into the building for programs and more, then it will be worth the risk. And it will be possible to show colleagues and administrators the value of that risk with higher programming numbers.

Serving these teens may require riskier programming tactics, but remember that the library should serve everyone in the community, whether it's a public or school library. Never be afraid to remind community members or administration that these new audiences are part of the library's service population.

But there are libraries where teens never set foot into the building. Librarians in these facilities may hear teens shouting out to each other as they walk outside the building, so they must be close by. How do those teens get brought into the library? Moreover, how does the librarian convince the administration to start a teen program in a building that's never had anyone between the ages of thirteen and eighteen walk through its doors?

Ray Lusk, the events coordinator at the Madison Library District (Rexburg, Idaho) was the first librarian to host teen programming in his library. He went all the way from zero programs to teens spending the night. He created a teen summer reading program and eventually convinced administration to allow him to host an overnight teen lock-in. Ray knew to talk to the teens in his library's community. That helped him prove to his administration that teens needed their own programming at the library. Ray also knew that he had other allies within the community who could help him advocate for teens. By reaching out and collaborating with businesses and other nonprofit organizations in his community, he was able to take risks and strengthen his teen program with support from outside the library.

Ray Lusk Discusses Risk in Teen Programming Start-Up

What began as a question about an underserved population in the Madison Library District has blossomed into a wildly successful teen summer reading program. The Madison Library District in Rexburg, Idaho, serves a population of about thirty-two thousand people, including eleven thousand K–12 students. The children's summer reading programs have been an integral part of library services for decades. However, the library had never had a summer reading program, or any regular programming for that matter, for adolescents before we organized their first summer program five years ago.

The Rexburg area is largely agricultural and nearly 40 percent of the library's service population resides outside the city limits. This led us to question whether teens would come to the library for programming. Another difficult question to answer was whether the teens needed, or even wanted, their own summer reading program. We determined in 2005 that the only way to answer those questions was to take a risk, and organize the first teen summer reading program at our library.

Once we were determined to make the program happen, we had to figure out who would run the program, how it should be structured, and how it should be funded. After much discussion among the youth services staff, it was decided that the program would reward teens ages twelve to eighteen based on the number of pages they read, and whoever read the most would receive a grand prize at the conclusion of the program. The library director gave us a budget of just three hundred dollars for the program. We also solicited input from the pages at the library, whose insights were invaluable. After all, they were currently or recently teens themselves. With their help, we planned a final after-hours party with free food and games to end the program.

Because the entire program was uncharted territory, we had no idea what to expect. The library had never had any YA programming of any kind prior to this year. It was a major risk. What would happen if it flopped? Would we ever try again? Would it be a waste of our time? We took the risk. We were so excited to have approximately ninety teens at our final party and a total of two hundred teens sign up for the summer reading program. Wow! What a successful first year!

We never would have known how many teens we could reach had we not tried. But now we faced another question. Could we do it again? What had we done to make the program a success? For the past five years we have modeled our program on the same basic structure—the person with the highest page count winning a prize, and a final party for all. However, each year we learn more about what our teens want and each year we make changes to accommodate those needs.

In the years since the program started, the number of teen participants has remained largely static. This last year, the participation more than doubled to 442 teens who signed up for the program. What made the big difference? Last spring, a few of us who work with teens decided to try reaching out to teens at the local public high schools and junior high during their lunch period. At the time, we didn't know whether those visits would have an effect on our summer reading statistics. The impact of those visits was more than we could have imagined.

To accommodate our growing program, we reached out to community organizations that have recognized our success and the importance of our programming. They now contribute many of our prizes at no cost to us. By partnering with other organizations, all parties receive benefits. Sponsors experience an increase in visibility, while the library can offer greater incentives to participants.

This past summer we decided to have weekly activities. Some weeks we invited guest presenters, others featured a quick craft. The craft-based activities totally flopped, but presenters who were interactive were very successful. Teens in every community are different, so you may find that an activity that was successful in a nearby community just doesn't appeal to your teens. Our teens, we learned, would rather have an improv comedy group perform and teach them about acting and expressing themselves, than make masks and have a masquerade. How did we learn that? By taking a risk and trying.

Did we take a risk? Yes. Did some risks flop? Yes. But the most important thing is that no matter the outcome, we learned what worked and what didn't, and we can apply those lessons in the future to better serve our teen population.

"Only those who risk growing too far can possibly find out how far one can go."—T. S. Eliot

BEST PRACTICES FOR RISKY PROGRAM PLANNING

Ray Lusk offers a good example of how one library staff member can build a strong teen program. But how does a librarian really get things going? How does a librarian encourage feedback and gain support from administration and colleagues? Consider a scenario where a library's teen advisory board (TAB) members have brainstormed creative new programming, but the librarian is not sure how to bring those ideas to fruition. The teen librarian needs to gain support from the administration, make sure the teens are prepared to plan and implement the program, be able to stand up for teens with coworkers and administrators, and get the word out about the success of teens. More specifically the teen librarian should undertake the following initiatives.

1. Invite her supervisor and administrator to talk with teens or the TAB. So much of the work that young adult librarians do can be improved through relationship-building. From a distance, an administrator may think of teens in the library as a rowdy group of unruly kids. But if placed face-to-face with a group of dedicated, open, honest teens who want to make the library a better place, it will be hard to miss understanding how the TAB can fulfill the needs of an important part of the library's community. Set up a meeting with an administrator and the TAB or a group of neighborhood teens. Make sure the teens know to be on their best behavior. Host a practice session with the teens to help them prepare for the meeting. The more focused they are, the better they'll be able to communicate their ideas, and any administrator will be more willing to listen.

2. Be a project manager. Teens have great ideas, but it's crucial that a librarian help them shape those ideas into something feasible that fits into the framework of the library. Help teens understand the steps they need to take to get their ideas heard and executed. Be honest with them; if their ideas won't work, let them know and tell them why. It may seem risky to be honest, but the teens will respect that honesty.

3. Help the group come up with other options if an idea is too risky, and be prepared to stand up for teen ideas when appropriate. Explain to teens how the library operates and how they can fit their ideas into its plans. It's not an easy task, but it's a great opportunity to put the ideas of youth development—giving teens the opportunity to be a part of planning and implementing activities they participate in—into action.

Kate Pickett of the Johnson County Library was once charged with working with her TAB to create a teen space in the library. As the young adult librarian, part of her job was to represent the opinions of teens when speaking with her administrators. "I am not afraid to voice my opinion if I think administration is making a decision that would negatively impact teens," she told this book's authors. The TAB was given complete artistic control of the space by the board of directors. However, after the group decided on a mural for the wall, the library board came back and vetoed the teens' ideas. Kate stealthily represented the teens at the next board meeting and explained why it was important to empower the TAB and respect their opinions. Eventually, the board, Kate, and the TAB were able to come to a consensus that satisfied all interested parties.

4. **Celebrate success.** Taking risks practically demands demonstrating to everyone in the library and the community why the risk was worthwhile. Host an event to celebrate the success of the risky program. Invite the TAB, their friends and families, administrators, and the rest of the library staff. Ask one of the teens involved in the project to talk about what led to the successful completion of the program, and be sure that the library administration has an opportunity to thank the teens publicly for their hard work and dedication. Take plenty of pictures to document both the project and the final event or outcome.

OUTSIDE-THE-BOX RISK TAKING

It's risky to try a program that's never been implemented in the library. But taking risks in programming can find the library hosting an event or offering an activity that lines up with the library's mission in an unexpected way and that utilizes a new artistic, educational, or social medium. These kinds of programs can be controversial because they challenge user and staff notions of what is deemed an appropriate library activity. Programs like this come in all shapes and sizes; they might involve new technology that the library has never utilized before. They might celebrate the library as a central social meeting ground for neighborhood teens. And they might be fun, noisy, and not tied to school curricula. Programs like this could include library lock-ins, gaming events, machinima design workshops, break dancing instruction, and more. Planning and executing these programs can be simultaneously exciting, stressful, and exhilarating.

These programs require lots of preplanning and detail work, sometimes utilize a special guest, and should get support from all levels of library staff before they are executed. It's important to use the risk checklist (see appendixes B and C) before moving forward on these programs in order to anticipate reactions from the public or the library staff.

Stephanie Squicciarini, a young adult librarian at Fairport Public Library (New York), took a big risk by founding the Greater Rochester Teen Book Festival and planning its first year without finalizing a budget. To move forward without certainty of funding, she collaborated with the others in the library and community. They chose a date for the event, selected and booked a location, and began inviting authors. The event did get a budget eventually, and the first Greater Rochester Teen Book Festival went off without a hitch and was a hit with the teens there. The event is now in its fifth year, and teens are still loving it.

RISKY PARTNERSHIPS

Another great way to take risks in programming is to find partners. Collaborations with recognized cultural and social organizations increase programming credibility in the eyes of the audience and library staff. As a result, the work, activities, stress, tangible outcomes, and responsibilities related to the program are shared among the collaborators. Burdens of risk are even more relieved when partnering with a recognized community organization, such as an after-school program, historical society, community theater, and so on. Just be sure the partnership meets the needs of the teens and the library.

Partnerships can take many forms. Experts in local hospitals can be a great resource when it comes to talking to teens about health issues. Local radio stations might have DJs who could lead workshops for teens. Senior centers might provide volunteer opportunities for TAB projects. Local authors might offer free book discussions or talks to teens. Finally, after-school organizations are perfect partners that can help build audiences for new library programs.

Of course partnerships come with their own sets of risks. It can be risky to start a relationship in which the partners aren't all that familiar with each other and need to learn to trust each other's work styles and habits and respect different philosophies related to serving the community as a whole or teens. But although there are risks in these partnerships, they are often worth taking because they expand the possibilities for getting things done for teens and highlight the importance and value of library teen services.

When starting a new partnership with a community organization, begin with a small project so that the partners can get to know each other. Start by working with just one other organization or community member. That provides an opportunity for getting used to working with another agency and learning about what makes community partnerships work.

Don't forget that many cultural institutions and social organizations in the community may have youth outreach grants that require them to find partners. Many of these grants often include creating programming beyond the walls of the institution or bringing new audiences into their building. Either of these could be great educational and creative opportunities for teens to learn about another organization in the community that supports their needs. Plus these kinds of shared programming ventures stand out on future grant applications.

PAD THE RISKS

With an understanding of the variety of risk-taking opportunities in teen library programming, it's time to look at some ways to build credibility and support for ideas with the administration before taking a risky leap. Remember that meeting any and all of the benchmarks that follow can help build support for a risky program and give the library administration the right level of confidence to know that it's OK to proceed with risks.

Get Support

Get support from everyone in the library, or as much support as possible. This support goes all the way from the staff on the front lines to the director, other administrators, elected officials, and more. The more support garnered, the better equipped a librarian can be to handle any issues that arise before, during, or after a program. Figure out what issues fellow staff members could face ahead of time and discuss them with colleagues. Simply talking about the program and brainstorming these issues with staff members is a great, easy way to win support. Ask opinions and encourage attendance at the program once it comes to fruition, so that they can experience the success.

Ask to speak to your board of directors or trustees about the program. When the invitation comes, be prepared. Know what needs to be said and how to say it. If asked to give a presentation, be sure to come with the appropriate handouts and technology needed to properly outline the particulars of the program. If possible, include direct quotes from teens in the presentation about why they think implementing the program is important. If there are pictures of past successes, include those as well. Remember, the better the librarian presents herself in front of colleagues, the more trust there will be in the decision making that goes on related to teen services.

Talk to the Teens

When it comes to advocacy, nothing is stronger than words coming straight from the horses' mouths. Get support from teens who come to the library or who are in the community. There may be opportunities for teens to speak to the director or elected officials about teen library programs. If this chance does arise, be sure to take time to prepare the teens. Coach them on what to say and how to say it. Give them insights on how their audience will react. Ask the teens to rehearse their talks during a TAB meeting to get them used to hearing themselves speak publicly. Don't take chances with winging it; this is the teens' opportunity to shine for the library and they should be ready for the spotlight.

Also ask teens to talk to their friends about the program. This can happen both in person and online. No one gives better PR for teen programming than teens themselves. Once a few teens endorse a program, others will follow. The administration will love it when the programming numbers increase due to teen word-of-mouth.

At the end of the program, tell the teens about upcoming programs, so they'll make a return visit. They are the greatest ambassadors to the rest of the teen community.

Promote the Risks

Regardless of whether or not your library has a public relations department, promoting a risky program is key to getting the word out and getting teens into the library. Be sure that everyone on the staff is aware of the program and can talk about it to teens, parents, and families who frequent the library.

Create fliers, handbills, or other print advertising to distribute to local schools and businesses and to post around the library. Give out the fliers during class visits to neighborhood schools, and be sure to leave copies in school administrative offices.

Be sure to blast the event through the library's social networking pages, such as Facebook or MySpace. If teens who are active at your library are your friends on a personal social networking account, include information on the event in your status update or send them a message. Ask TAB members or teen programming regulars to post the event in their own online communities. Contact local newspapers, TV, and radio about your program. This is an easy way to get the word out to both teens and their parents.

If there is time and money, brand the risk. Come up with a short, memorable umbrella title for the series of risky programs. Provocative headlines such as "Risk!," "Not What You Might Expect," and "Be Here Now" can become effective advertising slogans that grab the attention of teens who might not think of the library as a place where risky programming happens. Use the brand on all advertising. Teens, along with everyone in the community, will eventually come to recognize the brand.

Document Success

It's been a lot of work to create an awesome, risky program. Make sure to capture it to show all aspects of the program development and implementation to skeptical library administration—or to add it to your resume. Blogs, photos, and videos document the hard work that went into the risky program building. And documenting successes is crucial to securing future grant applications and partnerships. If pictures or video are a part of the documentation, get parental permission if you decide to publish any pictures of youth under the age of eighteen.

FINAL THOUGHTS

Defining the parameters of risky programming for libraries requires an understanding of the needs and values of teens, their caregivers, the community, and the library staff. Once teen librarians understand all of those pieces, it's time to take the first steps. Remember that even though administration and fellow staff members might not give the green light to try everything desired by teens at the library, most likely it will be possible to move forward on some aspects. Keep teens in mind at all times when planning any programs for them, as they are the best trump card when it comes to advocacy. Teen voices, combined with a librarian's communication skills, can help the rest of the library staff understand why risk is necessary in serving teens at the library.

5
Technology
A Risk Worth Taking

The risks involved in integrating technology into teen programs and services are many. They range from being willing to embrace social networking technologies and friending teens on those sites, to collaborating with teens on projects virtually, to working within a filtered environment in which teens might not be able to access all the information that they want and need.

Frances Jacobson Harris, a librarian at the University Laboratory High School Library in Urbana-Champaign, found that technology freedoms can both be a benefit and a challenge. She told the authors

> I'm a librarian at a public school for three hundred gifted students in grades eight through twelve, ages twelve to eighteen. I also team-teach a required computer literacy course sequence that includes information literacy skills components and ethical and responsible uses of communication and information technologies. Students and staff are given great amounts of personal freedom and responsibility, which can be both liberating and challenging.

In a YALSA-sponsored e-chat in August 2009, Liz Burns, the youth services consultant for the New Jersey State Library's Library for the Blind and Handicapped, said, "With technology, by the time people are comfortable with the risk the technology is so 2005."[1] Unlike risks that are a part of traditional library services, such as book selection, technology risks can sometimes be more challenging because those working with teens may be learning about new technology at the same time they are trying to integrate that technology into programs and services. As a result, it's not often possible to inform administrators and colleagues about all of the benefits (and pitfalls) of the technology until during, or even after, the technology has been implemented. That's risky. But if the pros and cons of going with a new technology before knowing everything about it, and w-a-i-t-i-n-g until all the pieces are weighed, the conclusion should be that waiting is a risk that will almost always lead to failure. By the time decisions are made, the technology won't be of interest any more, or may have changed so much that the research process needs to start over. However, if librarians are willing to take the risk and learn along the way, then failure is less of a certainty.

This chapter takes a look at some of the technology risks librarians working with teens have already taken, discusses why taking technology risks is worth the gamble, and provides some tips and tricks for being successful when considering, or implementing, a risky technology program or service.

THE RISKS OF GOING SOCIAL

Sarah Ludwig, head of teen and technology services for Darien Library in Connecticut, stated in a YALSA Blog post that

> When I learned that my Facebook presence was going to be included in the library's monthly e-newsletter, along with my Twitter, MySpace, and AIM accounts, I realized it would be pretty embarrassing for someone to visit my profile and see that I didn't actually have any friends from my community. So I took a plunge. I started friending kids. I included a note; you can do this on FB. The note said something like: "Hi, I'm the teen librarian at the Darien Library and I'm trying to get to know people in Darien. I know you don't know me, so if you don't want to accept me as a friend, I totally understand! But if you do, that would be great."[2].

For many librarians, friending teens in a Web-based social networking environment is risky. They worry that friending a teen might cross boundaries of personal space, both for the teen and the librarian. Being a teen's friend on Facebook, for example, might mean that a librarian will know more about that teen than she feels comfortable with. Librarians ask, "What if a teen posts something on her wall that lets me know she's up to an activity that I don't think is smart and safe? I don't want to be involved in a teen's life in that way, and I wouldn't have to worry about it if I don't become her Facebook friend."

But as Sarah Ludwig goes on to say, "It worked!" In what ways does it work and why is it worth the risk? Consider the following points:

By friending teens where they live online, it's possible to connect them to library programs and services without ever seeing them face to face. (Of course that's something else that seems risky—creating services that teens can use without every entering the library. More on that below.) Teens who would never come into the library can learn about materials, events, and even use resources straight from their virtual Web 2.0 spaces. No longer do libraries just meet the needs of teens who are traditional library users; they meet the needs of teens who are nonusers. As Sarah goes on to say in her YALSA Blog post,

> . . . the great thing about FB fan pages is that they really can be portals for a ton of information and content about your library. You can post photos and videos, list upcoming events (which you can blast out to all of your friends, and get them to RSVP to), post news items, and list basic information, including a link to your library's website and your email address and IM username. You can send messages to all of your fans with the click of a button, too.

Learning about privacy settings on social networks, and taking time to carefully determine what settings to use, are key aspects of their successful use. All users should spend time figuring out who sees what information within a socially networked environment. When librarians use Facebook and other networks of this sort with teens, they can model the best way to establish privacy settings. A librarian might set up an account so that only personal adult friends get to see photos and wall postings. She can specifically block teens from seeing information that could cross into personal space. The librarian can also suggest that teens spend time looking into their own privacy settings to help guarantee that they understand what their librarian friends do and do not have access to.

The methods that librarians use to connect with teens in social network environments differ. Sarah sent messages to teens in her community asking them to friend her. But Frances Jacobson Harris says, "I never initiate a friend request, but I will accept friend requests from students."

What's key is not to shy away from the risk because it exists, but figure out the best way to embrace the risk in a particular setting.

It's important to decide the best way to friend teens online; it's also important not to hide the decision. For example, if the decision is to let teens take the initiative in requesting friendship of the librarian, then don't hide the fact that friending a librarian is a possibility. Inform teens that the teen librarian is available in social networks and welcomes them to make connections. Making the decision is only the first step; it's important to let teens in the community know what that decision is and how they can take advantage. It's pretty easy to say, "I'll friend teens on Facebook if they ask me to, but they never ask me so they must not be interested." But if teens don't know about the possibility, how can they do the friending?

BEING PREPARED FOR THE SOCIAL RISKS

Part of making good decisions when it comes to teens and social networking is in making sure that there are policies in place that support risk taking. At a recent meeting of librarians talking about integrating Web 2.0 into their programs or services, there was a discussion about the value and need for all librarians in the library system to become bloggers. This made some staff members nervous because they didn't feel comfortable taking the risk of posting to a library-sponsored blog. Staff worried that the wrong thing might be said. In response to their concerns, one of the technology staff members stated, "You know, we trust you to say the right thing when working on the reference desk or on the circulation desk. The blog is no different. Use the same judgment on the blog that you would in a face-to-face library environment and you will be fine."

That seems like a very clear and easy way of looking at librarian blogging. But what about the more general kinds of conversation that might appear on something like a Facebook wall or in a Twitter post? That's where the need for a social media policy, or social media guidelines, comes into play.

Ellyssa Kroski wrote, "A social media policy can help establish clear guidelines for staff members who are posting on behalf of the organization as well as employees with personal social media accounts. There are also standards being created for users, letting them know what's acceptable to post to an organization's blog and community pages."[3]

This policy, or set of guidelines, not only can outline how library staff can and should make smart decisions when it comes to using social media in the library, it also guarantees that librarians are not constantly re-creating the wheel of acceptability in the social networking setting. One of the benefits of guidelines over policy is that guidelines, since they do not have to be voted on by an official governing body, can be flexible and change fairly easily. If technology changes, the guidelines can be updated quickly to reflect that change. Don't forget that social media policy, or guidelines, can also act as a framework from which to work when talking with teens about the library's social networking presence. The document that is developed could be a very useful way to start conversation with teens about how to behave when in online environments. Maybe it would even make sense to have teens help develop the guidelines; that way, teens have the chance during the development process to learn why a policy is important and about the issues that the library needs to consider to ensure use of social networking is successfully implemented.

WHY TECH-BASED COLLABORATION IS WORTH THE RISK

High school librarian Jamison Hedin started using collaborative technologies in her first year in her job. She told the authors,

> Last year I worked with a member of the English department to use Google Documents for a multi-phase literary criticism project. It was the first time Google Docs was used in our district, really the first time any Web 2.0 tool was used by the students in the course of completing a school project.

Often, being the first to try something new in a library is a risk. When it comes to technology, the risks can increase. When it comes to using technology to get work done with or for teens, the risks can increase even more. For example:

- Colleagues who are already uncomfortable using technology may not want to demonstrate their lack of skills to their peers within a collaborative environment. Although a technology-based collaborative experience might be the perfect way to get work done, it's hard to see that when that experience can also show what someone doesn't know.

- Using Web-based technologies to collaborate makes the work—whether or not it involves teens—extremely transparent. Imagine using a wiki to plan a new program or service with teens, and imagine that the wiki is available to anyone on the library staff who is interested in the project. That means that any staff member can see the comments and questions teens ask along the way, they can see how the teen librarian interacts with the teens online, and they might see what teens have to say about the library and the library staff. That can seem very risky to some.

Of course teen services is all about collaboration. Isn't that what youth participation is: collaborating with teens in order to develop the best programs and services for them? It's only natural then that technology be integrated into a library's collaborative teen efforts, even if it is risky. Some reasons:

- For many teens, technology-based spaces are where they live and work. They are comfortable using technology to collaborate, even if a librarian is not.

- Using wikis, Google Docs, and so on makes it possible to easily collaborate from inside and outside of the library. A teen can log in to her Google Docs account, click on the link to the document she and her peers are working on in the library, and edit it. She can do that at home, at a friend's house, at school, at the library, or even while traveling with her family.

- Because collaborative technologies provide access from almost anywhere, that means librarians can collaborate this way with teens who might never come into the library or might not have any idea about what the library provides. It's a perfect way to get teens involved in library programs and services, and could lead to members of the age group actually walking through the library's front door.

- Using collaborative technologies provides those involved in the project complete documentation of the process. With wikis and Google Docs for example, it's possible to look at a history of revisions and changes. That means that librarians and teens can return to the work done previously as a way to plan for a next version of the project or to simply remind themselves of what it took to get to the final product.

Collaborating using technology-based tools is a fairly new possibility for librarians working with teens, and while it can be risky, it is definitely something that should be fully embraced. All teen participation activities don't have to move into the technology-based environment. Start with one that seems like an easy fit. Perhaps in planning a new program with teens, it would make sense to use a wiki so teens can brainstorm ideas about how the program will work, what needs to be accomplished to get it off the ground, develop a time line, and so on. Get feedback from teens and then maybe add something new to the technology-based collaboration repertoire. Taking one collaborative risk at a time can be effective and help move things forward.

GETTING STARTED WITH TECHNOLOGY RISK TAKING

One way to think about getting started in technology risk taking is to compare the technology programs and services already provided in the library with what might be, to some, a risky technology-based service.

When promoting the new technology-based program or service, it's possible to present the idea to colleagues, administrators, and community members by comparing what's being suggested to something already provided by the library. Presenting the idea this way helps those who need to buy in to it with a way to feel comfortable with the overall concept because it's not entirely new; it's just a variation of what's already provided. Which means it's a lot less risky than it appeared at first glance.

Consider the examples below.

Booktalking

Traditional: class visits in which the librarian promotes books available for checkout at the library

New technology-based version: book trailers (similar to movie previews) that teens produce about favorite books, new books, and other materials in the library collection

Selling points: Class visits, which often focus on booktalking, usually are provided on a limited basis and in many instances the librarian doesn't get to see all teens in the community during these visits. Also, it's often difficult for the teen librarian to get out of the library in order to visit schools. Web-based book trailers are available to anyone and are available twenty-four hours a day, seven days a week. The library and the librarian therefore are able to reach more teens than with traditional class visits. Web-based book trailers also give teens the opportunity to get involved in selling materials to their peers. In many cases teens prefer the word of their friends over the word of a librarian (or another adult). With teens as the producers of the book trailers and as "booksellers," more materials might get into the hands of members of the age group.

24/7 Book Discussion

Traditional: monthly book discussion group in which teens read and then discuss the same book

New technology-based version: Web-based book discussion using Goodreads, Facebook, or another social networking site

Selling points: Teens who might never come into the library may participate in a social-network-based book club. These teens might live too far from the library to be able to get to the facility when the face-to-face book discussion is going on. Or they may be involved in other activities at the same time the book group takes place. Or they may simply feel uncomfortable in a face-to-face group talking about books. Not only are Web-based book discussion groups more available to teens than face-to-face groups, they give teens the chance to talk about the book without committing to a specific time. Teens in the online book discussion can converse with peers about the book as they are reading, posting thoughts and questions about what's going on in a story at any time day or night. This ongoing conversation provides great opportunities for analysis and understanding of text as well as for getting to know the viewpoints of others related to a reading experience.

Learning Research Skills

Traditional: classes for teens on using library research tools

New technology-based version: screencasts on using library research tools that are produced by teens and the librarian, and are available within a library's Web presence

Selling points: As with the two examples above, screencasts provide more teens with information about using library resources that can be accessed twenty-four hours a day, seven days a week. Screencasts also provide teens with the opportunity to learn about using a specific library resource, such as databases, exactly when they need it—for example, when working on a science project. These videos also give teens the chance to pause during the viewing and try something out for themselves, and to re-watch a section in order to better understand the concepts presented. Also, when teens create screencasts, they have the opportunity to cement their understanding of using a particular library research tool because they have to learn exactly how the tool works in order to teach others, and they have to explain how the tool works in a way that is clear to those who watch the video training.

Creative Writing Groups

Traditional: weekly meeting at the library where teens write stories, poems, and so on

New technology-based version: teens use Twitter and wikis to write and then edit stories, poems, and so on

Selling points: The Many Voices project provides a perfect example of why this type of activity is an excellent way to help teens in creative writing.[4] Many Voices brought middle school students from around the world together to write a story via Twitter. Each classroom that participated in the project added a chapter to the story using several

140-character entries on Twitter. Once each school added their Twitter chapter, the story moved onto a wiki where students edited their writing, added images, and eventually published the complete text using the Web-based self-publishing site Lulu. Teens who participated in this project were able to collaborate worldwide and see their work develop day-by-day. They were also able to learn writing and editing skills as they revised on the wiki. The final step of self-publication helped guarantee that teens were invested in the work because they knew that the story would be available around the world for others to read and own.

Booklists

Traditional: theme-oriented booklists printed and distributed at the library and in schools

New technology-based version: website that includes book reviews and videos of teens talking about books

Selling points: Going to the Web to produce and publish theme-oriented book and materials lists for teens is cost efficient and makes for easy upkeep. With a Web-based version, print lists no longer need to be copied and physically distributed; when a book is no longer available, the Web version of the list can be updated. (No more previously photocopied lists being thrown in the trash.) Don't forget too that with a Web version of theme-oriented lists, teens can have a strong presence in the creation of the content. An example of this is the *Stuff for the Teen Age 2009* published by the New York Public Library.[5] After eighty years, the library went from a printed booklet of best books of the year for teens to a website in which videos of teens talking about a wide array of materials are included.

BUT THEY'LL NEVER COME TO THE LIBRARY!

As the examples above demonstrate, technology enables libraries to provide services to teens who might never come into the library. This can seem risky because the traditional framework requires teens to come inside the building to participate in what's offered. But providing services only to teens that visit the physical library space is actually more risky than providing off-site services. That's because cell phones, handheld devices, laptops, etc. are all tools teens use to communicate, participate, and collaborate. Libraries need to be part of the use of these tools or risk being ignored by teens entirely.

Why does it seem risky to serve teens virtually and to make it possible that teens who use the library's virtual services may never come into the building? Is it because librarians:

Think they won't have the statistics necessary to sell their programs and services to the administration, colleagues, and the community? If so, then it's important to realize that Web-based services bring the ability to collect usage data. For example, if Facebook is used for teens to discuss the development of library programs, the teen librarian can gather numbers related to the number of Facebook fans the library page has and also the number of teens that participate in discussions on the topic.

Are uncomfortable with the technology? If so, then it's important to gain comfort in order to serve the teen population effectively. That might mean asking a teen for help on learning how to use the technology or giving teens the chance to set up the virtual service with the teen librarian acting as mentor and coach. It's actually not necessary to understand all facets of how a technology works in order to integrate it into teen programming and services. Taking the risk of learning the technology from teens along the way can be beneficial. Teens are empowered by helping the librarian learn the technology, and the librarian as learner has the chance to ask questions of teens that help them to think about what the technology actually does, how it works, and then to articulate their understanding of the technology. It becomes a learning situation for all involved.

Believe that services can only be offered effectively in face-to-face environments? If so, know that in the social networking and Web 2.0 world there are lots of examples of positive collaborative and reading experiences available. For example, it's possible to find active book discussion groups on Goodreads in which teens and librarians talk together about books—just like in a face-to-face book discussion group.

Think that by providing virtual services teens will never, ever come to the library? It's possible that they won't. But there are teens who don't come to the library when the focus is on face-to-face services. Therefore, why not look at providing virtual services as an opportunity to serve teens who might never use the library otherwise. Think of it as adding another library branch—a virtual branch. When teens interact with the library online, they are, in fact, coming to the library. It's just a different way of thinking about it. Finally, if teens learn to enjoy what the library has to offer virtually, they may end up being more inclined to visit face-to-face than if they have no experience with the positive impact the library can have on their lives. It's also important to remember that a program or service can include both face-to-face and virtual components. For example, the library might sponsor a red carpet film festival in which the book trailers that teens created for the Web are shown. Teens who created the videos, those who are interested in film, those interested in books, and so on, may all attend the festival and some of these teens might walk through the library doors because they liked the book trailers they saw on the Web.

Libraries need to be where teens are. Where many teens are today is online, on handhelds, e-book readers, smart phones, and portable gaming systems. Risk-taking librarians will create new service points just by being in these spaces with their teens. But there won't be risk in making sure teens have what they need from the library within the environment they are most comfortable using. That's not risky because that's just good service.

DOES FILTERING MAKE TECHNOLOGY LESS RISKY?

For some institutions, filtering is a good way to limit technology risks. The concept is that if we filter teen access to content on the Web, then teens won't be exposed to the "bad" stuff out there and will therefore be safe. However, in reality, by using filtering in a library setting, the risks could be greater than if teens were given open access to Web-based resources. Why? Because in a filtered environment, teens are not given the chance to be confronted by content that might be scary or danger-ous. And they aren't given the opportunity to access the problem content within a setting with people who can help the teen understand why the content could be dangerous, scary, or inappropriate for viewing. We need librarians, teachers, and parents to be willing to discuss with teens the pitfalls and positives of using technology successfully.

Teens do need opportunities to explore Web-based content in safe environments. But sometimes it might not be possible for a library to go without any filtering. What's a librarian to do in those instances?

- Work with the administration and technology staff to gain the ability to manage the filtering process. For example, maybe the teen librarian can turn off the filtering when working with a teen who needs more complete access.

- Have conversations with teens about why access might be filtered and what they need to know when using unfiltered computers. Talk to teens about how to keep themselves safe while online and include information about privacy settings on social network sites and ways to inform adults when finding something that could be considered inappropriate.

- Create materials about Web safety that teens can access in the library. For example, produce screencasts that show teens how to access privacy settings in Facebook. In the screencasts, discuss why it's important to access these settings and how they can be used effectively.

- Inform colleagues, administrators, parents, and tech-nology staff about the risks inherent in limiting access. Make sure they have access to the latest research on teens and technology and what that says about whether or not teens are truly in danger when provided with full, unfiltered access to the Web. (See appendix E for a list of resources on this topic.)

- Keep up on local, state, and national laws (and proposed legislation) related to access social networking and Web

2.0 resources in schools and libraries. For example, in October 2008, as a part of the Broadband Improvement Act, the U.S. Congress passed a law that included the need to teach Internet safety in schools. State legislatures have passed similar laws. Knowing about these can provide opportunities for promoting the need for unfiltered access in schools and libraries—because it's not easy to teach Internet safety when access to the materials which may be deemed unsafe is blocked. (See appendix E for a list of resources on this topic.)

Filtering can make librarians feel like they are keeping teens safe, when in actuality it is a false sense of security. It can even be seen as a *see no evil, hear no evil, speak no evil* framework, because in a heavily filtered environment the librarian doesn't see teens using websites that might be dangerous or problematic. She doesn't hear teens talking about these websites because they aren't allowed to access them in the library. And she never has a chance to talk with teens about them because they aren't a part of the everyday library experience. That's not an effective way to support teens in learning how to be safe and smart online. Instead it's more effective to give teens the chance to access what might be problematic resources in the library and then not shy away from talking with teens about what they are seeing and doing on the Web. Give teens the chance to ask questions about technology as they use it.

THE VALUE OF TECH-BASED RISK WHEN IT COMES TO COLLEGIAL RELATIONSHIPS

It can't be stated strongly enough that by taking risks with technology, librarians are serving teens in the way they need to be served. It's also important to take technology risks in order to guarantee that librarians serving teens know what's going on in the teen world. In an October 2009 YALSA Blog post, high school librarian mk Eagle wrote,

> It's a sobering thought to realize you might miss an important event if the bulk of the organizing and promotion takes place on a social networking site you don't use. And for many of us working in libraries, moments like these should be a wake-up call: if your district, school or branch prohibits social networking use, you're missing out.[6]

For example, librarians not using social media tools might have missed when Neil Gaiman worked with the BBC and Twitter users to write a story that was then turned into an audiobook.[7] This activity was a great opportunity for librarians to connect teens with a favorite author via a social networking platform. Similarly, those librarians not using social networking tools might not realize that publishers and library-related vendors regularly give away books and tools using Twitter. For example, in late November and early December 2009, YALSA offered free tickets to the Midwinter Games, Gadgets, and Gurus event to library school students. All that library school students needed to do was tweet. Those not on Twitter missed out on a great opportunity.

It can be risky to integrate technology into library programs and services. But it's just as risky—if not more so—to not integrate. Not using technology ends up being risky both in terms of providing programs and services and in being effective in the job. Take the risk of using technology instead of the risk of inaction. The teens will respond and your services will improve.

NOTES

1. Linda W. Braun, "Risk in Teen Services—the Transcript," YALSA Blog, http://yalsa.ala.org/blog/2009/08/06/risk-in-teen-services-the-transcript.

2. Sarah Ludwig, "The Amazing Power of Facebook," YALSA Blog, http://yalsa.ala.org/blog/2008/11/19/the-amazing-power-of-facebook.

3. Ellyssa Kroski, "Should Your Library Have a Social Media Policy?" *School Library Journal*, October 1, 2009, www.schoollibraryjournal.com/article/CA6699104.html.

4. Many Voices on Twitter, www.twitter.com/manyvoices.

5. The New York Public Library, "*Stuff for the Teen Age 2009*," www.nypl.org/books/sta2009/.

6. mk Eagle. "Not on Facebook—Not Invited?," YALSA Blog, http://yalsa.ala.org/blog/2009/10/15/not-on-facebook-not-invited.

7. "Twitter an Audio Story with Neil Gaiman!," BBC Audiobooks America Blog, www.bbcaudiobooksamerica.com/TradeHome/Blog/tabid/58/articleType/ArticleView/articleId/110/Twitter-an-Audio-Story-with-Neil-Gaiman.aspx.

6

Selling Risk to Administration and Colleagues

The first five chapters of this book defined what risk in libraries can look like in terms of collections, programming, and technology. The level of risk for each differs from library to library and from community to community, and only the librarian is able to gauge how risky a project will be for his particular library. This chapter explores how to set those risky ideas into motion.

Risk taking in libraries doesn't happen overnight or with just one person, and too often a risky idea or project comes to a standstill because the risk taker didn't ask others for help. Garnering support from library administration and colleagues for a risky idea can be a scary challenge, but it's an important step to take to ensure a project's success.

There are several different theories, issues, and methodologies to consider when pitching a risky project to administration and colleagues. What we provide here are a series of tried-and-true tips and ideas for librarians to consider before jumping off. Each risky project will require its own risky plan. Therefore, the risk taker may not need to use all of these steps. Or the librarian may need to rearrange the steps in order to fit the needs of a particular project. Money, politics, interpersonal relations, and overall strategic initiatives may be at play and should be carefully and sensitively considered when making a pitch to administration or colleagues for a risky endeavor.

STAY POSITIVE

Conveying positivity and dedication for teens and the library is the single most important skill everyone needs to master to ensure support from administration and colleagues for any project. It may sound silly, but it's much harder for an administrator to say no to a happy, empowered, sincere, enthusiastic face than a grumpy one. It should inform every aspect of your pitch from early information-gathering to the final presentation.

However, in many cases, this is easier said than done. Both large- and small-scale projects can be tremendously complex, rife with roadblocks, and can induce gigantic levels of stress for the involved parties. If it becomes hard to remain positive about a project, here are some tips librarians can consider to get back on track:

- Take a deep breath.
- Step back and look at the big picture.
- Take a break.
- Remind yourself why taking on the project is a good idea.
- Consider who will benefit from the project: teens? the library? library staff?
- Talk with a colleague.
- Ask for help!

While these tips may not be surefire solutions, they can help the stressed-out staff reflect on why their risky project is important to teens, themselves, and the library. Then take another deep breath and move onward!

TEN STEPS FOR SELLING RISK

As already stated, the road to risk is paved with politics, roadblocks, and more. But if the risk is well-planned, there can be rewards in the end for everyone. Here are ten important steps to take when preparing to pitch a risky idea.

1. Align the Risk with the Mission of the Library

Does your library have a mission or strategic plan? Is there a way that the risk can be embedded into part of a current library project, or does it complement past or upcoming initiatives? Making this simple match can help increase the priority of any idea, risky or not.

Some quick research will show that most libraries' mission statements include language about providing free and equal access, facilitating lifelong learning, and providing service to their communities. If finessed correctly, most risks could be justified within the boundaries of any library's mission.

The real challenge, however, is identifying how a risk might be aligned within an organization's long-range plans. These may be more specific, quantifiable goals like increasing online service or offering more aid to job seekers. Or they may be more general, overarching themes such as training staff to work better with youth, increasing the library's teen services presence on the Web, or creating a more solidly realized teen services department. These goals may not specifically mention teens, but there is probably a way for the teen-related risk to fit.

If this inroad can be identified early in the risk planning process, it will make activating the risk much easier. Also, when crafting the pitch for your risk, using the language created by the administration (which is probably also the audience) in the mission, strategic plan, long-range plan, and so on is a great way to morph the language of the pitch to match the communication style of your library.

2. Foster Relationships

Creating bonds by communicating with colleagues and administrators will lay a foundation for future opportunities. When it's time to request permission for the risk, chances are those administrators who feel connected to the requester will look more favorably upon the request itself. It's generally more difficult to say no when they trust, respect, and like the person. Sincerity counts, though, so don't overdo it. Just find ways to say hello and discover what you might have in common. An open, smiling face helps too.

There will always be people who enjoy negativity; we call these the naysayers. Naysayers find everything wrong with an idea and aren't open to change. Pinpoint these people early and establish relationships with them. Having a positive connection with a naysayer will help to reduce that person's criticisms. It also works to seek out ahead of time someone the naysayer admires or trusts—and see if this person would be willing to endorse the risk before presenting it to the naysayer.

3. Rally the Troops

Colleagues can be powerful allies. Movie companies hold free previews to create buzz before a film's release; fast food restaurants use test markets to try new menu items; publishers send out advance copies before a book's street date. Building excitement about a possible project before presenting it to management will lend credibility to the idea. In addition, running ideas by coworkers while they're still in the idea form allows for potential problems to surface. Having someone else pinpoint trouble areas before the decision maker has a chance to do so can be invaluable; it provides an opportunity to address the problems, fix them, or be ready to discuss them at the presentation.

It's also smart to speak with those who may be affected by the risk. However, be aware that the more people who are included, the more likely it is to slow down progress. Sara Ryan, the teen services specialist with Multnomah County Library in Portland, Oregon, said in an interview,

> When I think about risks that haven't worked out, the reason for the failure isn't typically in the nature of the risk itself, which is usually not around trying something new or changing the way a program works, but rather about the way in which I tried to implement the risk. For instance, if you try to move forward with an idea without consulting people who could be affected if the idea was put into practice, you're not being strategic about that risk. On the other hand, sometimes the process of trying to make sure all the stakeholders have buy-in (if you'll excuse the business-speak) makes it feel like the pace of change is glacial, which is especially frustrating to teens.

4. Find a Mentor

Mentors can help to navigate the way up the organizational hierarchy to administration. They can share their experiences in getting ideas passed and act as a sponsor when the risk is presented.

Find someone in an administrative position who will support the risk. She doesn't have to be a teen services specialist, but she should be supportive of risk taking and of teen services. Ask this person to sponsor the idea or to act as a mentor throughout the course of the project. This will act as a kind of insurance to pad the risk when presenting it to the administration.

5. Know the Audience

Whether you're presenting to one person or a group, find out what motivates them. Are they most concerned with the budget, the image of the library, or the teens themselves? Will the pitch presentation be for a task force with a specific charge? The library's board of trustees or senior management group?

Whoever it targets, the pitch presentation should be tailored to that audience in terms of quantity of information, language, visuals, and style. For example, if the presentation is for the library's senior management group who make the decisions but don't actually execute them, the presentation might need fewer small details and instead cover more big-picture impact. However, if the presentation is for the young adult department or another smaller group, there will no doubt be questions about the details of the project.

The key is to strike the balance between too much and too little information. Only the librarian will be able to gauge how exactly to proceed.

6. Be Aware of Timing

Money, politics, culture, and history all have an impact on the success of any risky project. Risk-taking librarians should be savvy of these factors when creating proposals and plans for new projects. For example, if the library has just undergone a series of major budget cuts, it's probably not the best time to propose a large, expensive project. Instead, perhaps it's best to propose a smaller, less expensive project and hold off on the larger one until better financial times.

Also, it's important to be aware of what's happening culturally and historically in the library. For example, if a library typically fund-raises in the spring for fall projects, then a project for the upcoming school year should be pitched in time for the library to raise money for it. That said, if technology is a part of the risky endeavor, think carefully about the time frame required to implement the technology in a meaningful way. If pitching a tech-based idea that needs to move quickly to take advantage of the technology, then the pitch might need to happen at a nontraditional time and it will have to be clear in that pitch that the planning and implementation need to be on a fast track.

Furthermore, if the library has already announced a major initiative or campaign that can be tied to the risky project, the risk-savvy librarian should look for inroads to connect exciting risky ideas to what the library is already doing. For example, if the library has launched a job readiness campaign for adults, why not brainstorm with teens about what their job prep needs are. Should there be a resume-writing workshop for teens? A program on financial planning? Materials for the teen collection on job readiness?

The risk-savvy librarian should also be aware of the timing of the pitch itself. Is the person receiving the pitch open to having someone walk into her office? Does a meeting need to be set up with a senior management group or board of trustees? Will the pitch be made at a staff meeting?

Finally, how long will the pitch-giver have to present? Risk-taking librarians should be fully aware of time constraints and plan their presentations accordingly. Presentations should never, never, never go over time, unless they're in the final, crucial decision-making moments or if there is heated interest and conversation seems to be going strong. Even if it's the latter, risk takers should remain aware of the time and announce to everyone that time is up but they would be happy to continue if everyone else can stay.

At best, the presentation should be short, sweet, to the point, and full of memorable details. That way, the audience will be itching to contact the risk taker after the presentation with any follow-up questions.

7. Remember the Bottom Line

Remember that money and numbers count. In the pitch presentation, risky librarians shouldn't shy away from honestly estimating what the project will require in terms of dollars and staff time. That said, the librarian should be aware of what the library's capacities are and tailor the project to fit those factors.

Also, the risk-savvy librarian shouldn't forget to include how she will evaluate the risk once permission has been granted to take it. What statistics will be generated from the risk? Will it affect circulation? Program attendance figures? Class visit and tour statistics? Will there be a survey for teens to complete when they participate in the project? Will the project need an outside consultant to help with the evaluation?

Thinking through these important details and communicating them to colleagues will help speed up the decision-making process for any project, risky or not. It will also help increase the credibility and reliability of the risk taker, which will build the foundation for the library accepting more risky projects!

For more on risk financing, see the "Being Prepared" section in this chapter.

8. Tell a Story

After the risk presentation, it's important for board members and managers to have something tangible to share with others. Remember that they want to be recognized as risk takers themselves and as supporting this new venture, so give them a story they can tell afterward. Successful stories include:

- personal anecdotes
- information from patron feedback forms
- survey results
- comments on a blog
- case studies
- how the risk will aid in positive youth development (remember the Forty Developmental Assets)

However, don't overload them. Give them "takeaways"—little tidbits they can take away and repeat to others—but don't overdo it. A few quality anecdotes can be more effective than several mediocre ones.

9. Believe in It

Passion and excitement are contagious. Enough said.

10. Be Prepared

Have a well-thought-out plan, which might include an elevator speech. An elevator speech condenses your plans and goals into a sales pitch that you can present in the time it would take for a short elevator ride with an administrator. Be sure to make your plan available in the format that is most appealing to your audience. (See the "Know the Audience" section.) Anticipate how questions will be answered, and make sure those answers are positive. Also, risk takers should think about how they can keep the conversation moving as questions arise. Anticipate any roadblock questions before the presentation so the conversations can avoid getting sidetracked.

Finally, if the risk taker isn't the one giving the presentation, the risky librarian should make sure that the presenter fully understands the nature of the risk and any tertiary information that may help her explain it.

BEING PREPARED

One of the best ways to be prepared for pitching risky ideas is to imagine all the questions and comments the administration will have, and how to answer them. Here are some examples.

What Will It Cost?

Invariably, if a risk is to be approved by any supervisor, manager, or board, one of the first questions will be, "How much will this cost?" These people must work within the confines of a budget, so it's possible they'll have to cut back in another area in order to finance this risk. The best answer to "How much will it cost?" is, of course, *nothing*. Proposing an idea that will be free to implement is a great way to garner support. But this isn't always possible, so here are a few ways to answer the big money question and to be prepared with a plan of action for funding.

> **Try to find funding outside of the library.** Many businesses have designated funds they are required to gift each year; take advantage of this by asking early and keeping relationships up with local companies' community relations coordinators.

Look to other government organizations. They may not be able to offer monetary support, but partnering with other organizations provides access to more nonmonetary resources and opens up a new base of potential patrons.

Take advantage of volunteers and Friends of the Library groups. Volunteers may be able to offset the money that would normally be spent on staff, while Friends groups are usually open to hearing new ideas for library programs and projects.

Emphasize how much return there will be on investment. How will the potential outcomes of this project outweigh any costs? Show how spending money on this risky project may actually save money later on.

Sometimes being "budget-challenged" can be advantageous. Budget deficits force libraries to be creative and pursue risky ideas they may have earlier shelved. Use this time to show alternatives to the status quo.

How Will It Be Perceived?

Public and school libraries alike must remain cognizant of their community. For public libraries this means the voting public, and for school libraries this means students and their families. Often this can result in a trepidation to try anything too risky. Further, library administration must think about how the risk will impact the community, and also how it will be perceived by the community. Perception and reality often diverge and it's important to think about both. In doing so, address plans for molding public perception and educating the community to the benefit of the project. Having steps already laid out for this will help to persuade the decision makers.

As mentioned in chapter 1, looking at a new project as something that can be launched in beta is a way to minimize risks. Consider pitching the risky activity to administrators as a pilot or test project. With a beta project, it's possible to discover exactly what teens and members of the community think about what's being launched and be smart about responding to actual concerns and informing everyone of the activity's value.

But We've Always Done It This Way—Why Change?

Small or monumental, change is difficult for many people and often keeps good ideas from turning into great realities. People who fear change must be reminded of all the good that has come from previous change in the library, such as offering video game programs or adding graphic novels to the collection. These ideas were a risk as well, but they've probably dramatically increased teen usage.

PUTTING IT ALL TOGETHER

So now what? The risky project is fully realized; the pitch presentation is planned, prepared, and tailored to a specific audience. Handouts and takeaways are finished. The presentation has been rehearsed in front of an audience. The pitch is ready to go! All that remains is setting up the time to give the pitch and figuring out who will be there and how much time there will be for the conversation.

As the beginning of the chapter stated, pitching your risky idea is probably the hardest step to take, but it's an important one that risk-taking librarians need to familiarize themselves with. And even if the risk isn't approved, learning and knowing these steps will help any librarian build credibility for future risky endeavors.

7

Risky Career Moves

What does it take to be smart when it comes to taking risks in one's career? How does passion to support teens affect next career steps? The authors of this book answer these questions by sharing their own career risks.

LINDA W. BRAUN: AN UNEXPECTED AND RISKY CAREER PATH

If you knew me in high school, college, or graduate school, you might be surprised by the path my career has taken and where I've ended up. It's not working in libraries that would be so surprising. What people might be surprised by is the fact that I work for myself and am very involved in a national organization, YALSA. Why the surprise? Because throughout all of my academic experiences, I was not one to speak up in front of a crowd or be much of a leader. I was someone who did the work when needed, but, while not exactly a follower, was not active in moving ideas and projects forward.

Now, however, that's what my life is about and it took making some risky decisions to get here. (Sometimes I didn't know the decisions were risky, but looking back I realize they were.)

I started my career as a children's librarian and that's where my career path was focused. I was happy planning and implementing children's programs, working on the collection, and managing small children's departments. Then one day the director of my library asked me if I wanted to add young adult responsibilities to my job. At that time I had a good rapport with all ages that came into the children's department—birth to age twelve—and it seemed to me that working with teens would be a natural step to take.

That was one decision I made that was definitely risky (and it was risky for the library director too). For one thing, just because I was successful with birth to twelve-year-olds was no guarantee that I would be successful with thirteen- to eighteen-year-olds. I'm very glad that the director took that risk with me—and that I took the risk he offered. But, as a wiser, older librarian knowing what I know now, I think that if offered that opportunity again I might ask many more questions before I said "yes." And I would do some research about what being a teen librarian really entails.

In many ways the risk paid off, because I didn't know as much as I might and the decision was a good one. It might have been a different decision if I had done research. So sometimes it's worth taking a leap of faith in your career. If your gut tells you it's the thing to do, that can be a good indicator of what you should do—even if you don't know everything about what the decision actually entails.

Of course your gut isn't always the best indicator for taking a risk, and while the opportunity that library director gave me changed the path of my career, other risky opportunities that I said "yes" to didn't have such a positive impact. For example, early in my career I was working at a library system where I was not a good match. I decided after just a few months to get out of the job and go somewhere else. I took a risk to leave a job that I hadn't been at for long because staying was just too difficult. That was a smart risk because I needed to get out. My happiness was more important than sticking it out.

The risk that wasn't so good was being willing to take almost any job to get out of the one I was unhappy in. I took a job in a special library that seemed like it was going to be great. It was in a field in which I was interested—television—and I thought I would be able to do some interesting projects. This was an instance in which more research would have been helpful. I should have looked more closely into what the job entailed and not simply bought the information presented by the interviewer. And because I had left another job within six months of starting, this time I didn't feel like I could leave before at least a year was up; two short-term jobs in quick succession on my resume seemed like a risk not worth taking. (I lasted eighteen months this time around.) So one good risk—leaving a job quickly after starting—limited my ability to take another risk. This was probably a time when I might have done some long-term thinking about how this all might play out instead of simply jumping from one bad job to another.

I did get back into teen services after that unsuccessful risk and realized as I was working in a small suburban library that I really liked many aspects of the job that revolved around managing projects and a department. I also enjoyed being involved in the community and planning and implementing projects with other town agencies. I was finding that while I loved working with teens, what I loved perhaps even more was being able to work toward making sure the services offered in a community were strong and effective. So, I took another risk.

A job became available for a youth services consultant for a state regional library agency. The job was something I really wanted to do, but there was a big risk: it was a temporary position to fill in for the current consultant who was on maternity leave. This time I did my research and talked with people in the know, including the woman on maternity leave. I was told that no one was sure what would happen at the end of the period for the temporary position. No one knew if the new mother would come back, and it was unlikely that there would be another job for me if she did return.

But I thought about my options. I thought about what I really liked to do. I thought about whether I'd likely have a chance like this again. And I decided this was a risk worth taking. I'm very glad I took it, because this is the risk that led to where I am today. I was fortunate that the person on leave decided not to come back to the job, so I was able to stay in the position for a few years. But even if I had only been able to remain in the position a few months, what I would have learned from it would have been so valuable that it was worth the risk. At the end of even a few months, I gained a set of skills that I wouldn't have been able to really gain in a traditional teen librarian position.

And then I probably took one of the biggest risks that one can take in their career: to start working for oneself. Giving up the steady paycheck of a "nine to five" is a big risk, but it's one that I knew was worth taking, even after I put a lot of thought into it. Here's how:

My job at the state regional library system was about to change. It wasn't going to be the job that I enjoyed and was good at. While I might enjoy what was coming next, I didn't want to wait around and find out. I was ready to do something new.

I wasn't going to go it alone. In the early days of having my own business, I had a business partner who had the same ideas, passion, and drive that I did. It was less risky and scary to be doing this with someone else.

There were people I already knew who would hire me. I'd gained credibility and contacts through my youth services consultant work, and several of those I had worked with were ready to hire me when I hung out my own shingle. I knew that for at least a few months I would be solvent.

There was a change coming in the library world and I thought I had something to tell people related to that change. Fourteen years ago, when I started my business, technology and the Internet were new in libraries. I was interested in those things and I was good at them. I was passionate about the topic and wanted to let others in on that passion.

I've been fortunate that by taking that risk to work for myself, I've been able to succeed, to continue to develop skills, to learn from others, and to have opportunities to take even more risks.

Throughout my career and the variety of risks that I've taken, I've learned that risks aren't always a good idea, but that if one is smart about risk taking, a lot of good can come from it. Risks shouldn't be taken lightly. But they can lead to great job benefits (and I don't mean insurance). Be smart about career risks, but don't be afraid to take them. Your work life is too important to shy away from taking the risk that will lead to a fulfilling career.

JACK MARTIN: STARTING IN LIBRARIES AT 13 AND NEVER LOOKING BACK

My mom first volunteered me to work in my local public library in Cornelia, Georgia, when I was thirteen. At first I thought to myself, "Jeez—I'm a big enough loser already. This is just going to make it worse." But somehow I found that I fit in well with the staff and the patrons, and before I knew it I had worked there part-time all through high school. From there, I moved to bigger systems in Athens, Georgia, Providence, Rhode Island, and eventually, to the New York Public Library.

There were risks taken at many different points and levels in my career, but here are some tips that I've learned both along the journey and the climb up the corporate ladder.

Be Mobile

One aspect of my career that my parents and peers have always considered risky was the fact that I've moved around to so many different libraries around the country. I've worked in several libraries in three different states: Georgia, Rhode Island, and New York. While I understood that there were risks involved including later retirement, job security threats, and stressful periods of readjustment, I wanted to get as much experience under my belt as possible. More important, I wanted to find the right job for me.

In hindsight, working in these different systems gave me an opportunity to try every aspect of library service. I worked in circulation, cataloguing, and at the information desks in the children's, adult, young adult, and reference rooms. I've worked in special collections such as the Heritage Room for genealogy in Athens, Georgia, and the art and music collection at the Providence Public Library. I've visited small, rural towns in south Georgia on a bookmobile that appears once per week, and, with just two staff people, I ran a library in a rundown firehouse in south Providence that used to get the windows shot out once a week. There was even one instance where I ended up running the entire library for a day when I was a teenager. All of these experiences had different effects on my career, but all of them helped shape it and gave me some great experience to add to my resume that have no doubt helped me get to where I am today.

For me, being mobile doesn't just mean moving from system to system or from state to state, but also moving to a new experience within a library system where I already worked. At the New York Public Library, I worked in two different branches and Teen Central before I moved into administration.

Throughout all of these moves, I've always looked toward a mentor who could give me insight on what might be the best options for me. For one of the more integral moves in my career at the New York Public Library, a very close mentor actually advised me *not* to take the new job because she feared it would affect my eligibility for another career path. I decided to make the change anyway, and to this day it was the singularly most important job change I could have made in my entire career. So while it was important to listen to the wisdom of others, it was also important for me to listen to my own gut.

Finally, even in my current position I try to be as mobile as possible. Each month I try to venture out of my office to visit teens and teen librarians in our libraries. It's a great way to connect with staff in our branches and the communities they serve, but it also keeps me in the know when it comes to the needs of the teens in our communities and what libraries can do to help fulfill them.

Embrace Change and Help Libraries Do the Same

Traditionally libraries are repositories for knowledge, so it can be hard for many of them—both large and small—to make and accept changes of any size. Change can come in the form of a new (or any) service to teens, introducing technology, or virtually anything. Depending on where a library stands on the willingness-to-try-new-things scale, I've learned that being an agent of change within a library can be sometimes miraculous, sometimes miserable, and sometimes both.

In interviews for any library job, I'm never afraid to ask my interviewers about how that particular library embraces change. I always use questions such as: Are they open to new ideas? Can the interviewer give an example of how a program moves from idea to reality? What's the administrative bureaucracy like? Are they open to allowing staff to try new ideas on their own? Or do they need to approve everything?

Any answers to these questions on the interviewer's part always gave me some great insight on how I could fit into the corporate culture of that particular library. That is, if the library was open to new ideas, then it was a good fit. If it just needed someone to carry on the previous librarian's work, it was probably not a good fit. I usually tried to stick with libraries that were open to change, because I knew that was the kind of environment I worked best in. If I landed in a position with no room for creativity, that's when I started the job-search process again.

On a final note, I always felt that new libraries or new teen spaces were always more open to try new ideas. The fresh environment helped ensure that staff morale was up, and I was offered a clean slate to begin building. I've always loved jump-starting teen services in new libraries. For example, when Teen Central at the New York Public Library opened, I immediately jumped at the opportunity to work in a new teen space that I suspected would set the standard for teen services for the entire system. The experience was fantastic: The head librarian was open to any idea I put on the table and helped the staff and the public support those ideas. We started the system's first teen advisory group, which became the blueprint for all teen services at NYPL. We had author visits galore and tried out some fantastic, outside-the-box programming designed by the TAB. It was one of the most creative, invigorating experiences that I've ever had in my career.

Big Risky Ideas That Need Big Funds

I've never been afraid to take risks in my work. However, I have had lots of administrators and directors who were afraid for the library to take the kind of risks I wanted to take. I discovered that learning how to strategically communicate my risky idea to the administration was almost more important than coming up with the awesome, risky idea, especially when big amounts of funds were required to make the idea work. Also, I knew there were most likely politics involved, and the trick to successfully sell my risky idea would lie in knowing the right channels, the right players, and the right timing.

Probably the riskiest initiative I've ever undertaken was Game On @ the Library for the New York Public Library. The project, which sought to expand an already-popular program from five libraries to eighteen, was expensive, involved the support of several different divisions, and added several new elements to the library's service that had never been tested before. It would impact staff at all levels, including development, staff in our branches, security, public relations, acquisitions, purchasing, marketing, collections, programming, and probably more.

Somehow, some way, our amazing director said yes, but not until I came up with a complete plan that involved conducting extensive research on video gaming and literacy, collecting statistics from our preexisting gaming programs to prove that gaming could increase both circulation and program numbers, and setting benchmarks and goals that predicted the outcomes of the project. It was hard work to gather everything, but in the end it paid off.

Game On @ the Library soft-launched in December 2007 in twenty-three libraries with a media event in the landmark Stephen A. Schwarzman Building on 42nd Street and Fifth Avenue in March 2009. The launch was a huge success, with more than a thousand gamers, players, journalists, media representatives, and curious onlookers. And Game On @ the Library lives on in even more libraries in our system, drawing thousands of teens, children, adults, and senior citizens into our libraries. The program has even expanded from open play to game design to teaching teens about careers in the gaming industry.

Other pieces of the project were less successful. Circulating games are now pretty much extinct on our shelves. We spent large amounts of funds on purchasing the games, but most if not all were stolen within the first few months of the project. While this outcome was disappointing, it did not have any negative impact on how I was viewed as a risk taker. Rather, it was seen as a successful test that the library did not have the funds to secure at the time.

Where I Am Now

I'm now involved in what could be the riskiest career move I've ever made. As of fall 2009, my job shifted from the assistant director of young adult programs at the New York Public Library to the assistant director of public programs and lifelong learning for children, teens, and families. Whereas my former job including planning programs and services for youth ages twelve through eighteen, my new one focuses on birth to parenthood. It's a huge leap, and at first I was pretty overwhelmed with the amount of work. I hadn't focused on working with children since my Providence Public Library days, and I certainly was out of touch with the programs and grant opportunities the library had been pursuing up until I stepped in. Furthermore, while I was familiar with the staff in our libraries who work with children, I hadn't been in direct contact with them about the services they provide. So I would need to do everything at once: familiarize myself with the content territory, get to know staff, learn about current projects, and keep everything moving in young adult programs at the same time.

Three months later, even though I haven't learned everything, my grip on the work is getting much stronger. We moved several major children's projects through the pipeline with tight deadlines, and I've had a chance to familiarize myself with the kinds of children's programming we offer, thanks to my staff. My next step is to immerse myself in the collections and the literature. Also in the upcoming year, I plan to venture out to children's programs as often as I go to teen advisory groups.

I think the hardest part about becoming an administrator is reminding everyone that you work with that even though you are an administrator, you're still that person who danced like crazy at the Anti-Prom or came up with the goofy pumpkin-carving idea during his first few weeks at a branch. It's a hard mold to break, but I try to push the envelope at least once or twice a day.

CONNIE URQUHART: THE RISKS OF SPEAKING UP

My mom loves to tell the story of going to a program at my elementary school where my class was singing a song, and hearing me loudest above the rest. She also loves to include the part about my voice being horribly off-key. Everyone could hear me belting out line after line in my tone-deaf singsong and there I was, having a ball.

I wish I had that kind of confidence now—don't we all? I stopped singing in front of others after an ill-fated audition for the school musical my freshman year of high school, but I've always been fairly confident in my work abilities and even more so in sharing my opinion on librarianship. I've worked in libraries for just eight years, but over this time I've taken many risks: some successful, some not, and most involving my mouth. (It seems that while I've stopped singing, I still can't keep the darn thing shut.)

An example: On Twitter, I've made the decision to mix my personal and professional lives. It's a risk because (a) I don't want my friends to get bored with lib-speak, and (b) I don't want to say something professionally inappropriate. With something as informal and immediate as Twitter, it's almost impossible not to. And? I did say something inappropriate, and I ended up issuing an apology to our library director. So that was a risk with negative results, and I'm much more careful now about what I say. But I still blend the two, because I think it's what makes me connect to my colleagues around the country: getting to know one another on a personal level. And here's a positive risk from the same story: when I apologized to my director, I also took a leap and asked to speak to her seriously about some issues that had been bothering me about my work environment, and how they contributed to my comment on Twitter. I was extremely nervous because I knew I was about to have a very personal conversation and I wasn't sure how satisfied I'd be with the results. In the end it was a difficult discussion, but I was so glad I did it. I think we both have a better understanding of each other now, and I think our conversation will lead to positive change within our organization.

So that would be my first piece of advice for new librarians: Don't be afraid to open your mouth. We are all entitled to our opinions, and I think people can see when you are coming from a truly genuine place. Other risky tips:

Pinpoint a fellow librarian who takes risks. Maybe it's a colleague, a supervisor, someone from YALSA, or someone you went to school with; it doesn't matter as long as you see him as a risk taker. Notice when he's doing risky things and what the results are. (I bet they're usually positive.) When you are contemplating taking a risk, go to this person for advice, knowing that he'll most likely encourage you. I have a few people like this in my life and they continually inspire me to be more open to things.

When in doubt about whether you should take a risk, ask around. Fear of the unknown can be debilitating, but chances are that someone somewhere has done it. Utilize the power of social networking to find someone who has taken your risk and can share her experience with you. Sometimes you don't even need to talk to the person; a little snooping into listserv archives, chat transcripts, or old blog posts will usually give you a start or point you in the right direction. I do this when selling a new idea to management, because it shows that we're not the first to try something (but thank goodness for those pioneers out there).

Ask yourself, "What happens if I don't?" So many times with risks we think about what might happen if we take it. Will the outcome be positive or negative, and what's the potential fallout? But we must also ask ourselves what kind of outcome inaction will cause. This is a question I ask myself often when it comes to collection development, especially when I think about buying something for the teen collection that may cause controversy. But when I ask "What happens if I don't?" the answer can be unsettling—that I could become a censor based on fear or a desire to avoid problems.

Finally, just remember that most things can be fixed. We may have to admit that we were wrong, but people respect honesty.

And on the topic of honesty, I must confess: I haven't stopped singing in public. I hadn't sung in front of others for many, many years, but I came out of retirement when I discovered Rock Band. I know I'm awful, but it's fun! And to all my former and future bandmates out there, I apologize.

8

Teens as Risky Role Models

Listen up, public librarians: the time when teens are most likely to engage in risky behavior is between the hours of three in the afternoon and eight at night.[1] That means that they've left school but may not be home yet. Those who view this as a curse may be associating teen risks with activities like drug use and unprotected sex. Yet those who view this as an opportunity know that not all risks are negative. A 2004 study by Students Against Destructive Decisions (SADD) found that teens who take positive risks are more likely to steer clear of the negative ones.[2] Sports, drama, and volunteering are all examples of teens putting themselves out there in a scary way that usually yields returns in the form of confidence and camaraderie. But don't think you're off the hook, school librarians (as if you thought you were!): many experts agree that taking risks is hard-wired into any teenager's brain. That means that even while teens' brains are most attuned to risk-taking in the after-school hours, librarians can still encourage positive risk taking during the school day.

CATEGORIES OF TEEN RISK TAKING

There are three main categories associated with positive risk taking for teens: life risks, school risks, and community risks.[3] Most librarians can expect to have a hand in at least two if not three of those categories. Here's how the SADD study breaks it down.

Life Risks

social—e.g., joining a club or group

emotional—e.g., asking someone on a date or sharing feelings with friends

physical—e.g., rock climbing

School Risks

academic—e.g., taking an advanced placement course

athletic—e.g., trying out for a sports team

extracurricular—e.g., running for student council

Community Risks

volunteering—e.g., helping the elderly or homeless

mentoring—e.g., working with younger children

leading—e.g., starting a business or charity

The best part is that engaging in these risky activities gives teens the opportunity to grow and the reinforcement they need to challenge themselves with even more positive risks. Conversely, negative risks can often lead to further harmful activities.

The Department of Health and Human Service's website for parents states

> Pre–teens and teens experience significant brain growth until they reach their early to mid-twenties. While this is happening, teens do not always accurately weigh the good and the bad of risks when making decisions. They need their parents and other caring adults to guide, encourage, and instruct them so they will choose healthy risks and avoid unhealthy risks.[*]

The SADD study found that approximately 80 percent of teens cite either their parents or their friends as the most likely to influence their decision making. That means that the other adults in their lives (i.e., librarians) must work with parents and peers to encourage healthy risk taking.

So what are some of those healthy risks libraries can offer? Here's a list of just a few. (All of these allow for teens to take risks in at least two of the categories mentioned above.)

- Put a teen in charge of leading a project. It could be short term, like organizing a display; or it could be long term, like coordinating an after-hours event.
- Plan a gaming program. Any time teens have to compete in front of others provides positive risk. Better yet, ask a teen to be the authority during a gaming tournament—let her create the rules, brackets, and so on. Or give teens the chance to teach adults in the community about gaming and demonstrate the positive aspects of gaming in teen lives.
- Host a talent show at which a variety of teens can stand up in front of their peers and adults in the community and show their skills and talents.
- Establish a teen advisory board and allow the elected officers to plan and facilitate the meetings and plan and implement library programs, services, and collections.
- Ask teens to help with programs for other age groups: a computer class for seniors, a haunted house for kids, hosts or ushers for music or author events.
- Create a homework club where teens tutor their peers and kids younger than they are.
- Provide an open atmosphere and really listen—teens may be ready to share something personal with you.

RISK-TAKING TEENS

The previous chapter illustrated how taking risks can aid career fulfillment. Similarly, there are benefits to teen risk taking too. Ninety-two percent of teen risk takers in the SADD study reported that they often feel happy. With that in mind, the following young people make great role models for taking risks.

Crystal R.

At the age of fourteen, Crystal Renn was told to lose seventy pounds if she wanted to be a top model. She did it through starvation and obsessive exercise, sometimes spending eight hours at the gym. At five feet nine inches tall, she weighed ninety-five pounds and was miserable. When she was told she still wasn't thin enough, she realized modeling in this way was never going to work for her. At eighteen, she decided that her health was more important, so she risked her career as a top runway model in favor of being a healthy plus-size model. She went from a size 0 to a size 12, and is now the highest paid plus-size model in the world. She talks about the risks she took in her book *Hungry: A Young Model's Story of Appetite, Ambition, and the Ultimate Embrace of Curves.*[5]

Crystal V.

Conservative Fresno, California, is the last place you'd expect to find the country's first transgender prom queen. But Crystal Vera defies expectations. In 2007, Crystal (formerly known as Johnny) was in some ways a typical senior: a dancer, a cheerleader, and excited about graduation. But being an open transgender high school student is anything but typical. Even riskier? The decision to run for prom queen. She knew that by taking a risk of this size there'd be a lot of attention thrown her way. What she wasn't expecting was the applause she received after she won—applause that continued in her classes and at lunch. In her acceptance speech, Crystal said, "Things are the way things are until someone changes it. I started seeing that someone has to be first."[6]

Ashley

She's a high school dropout. She's emancipated from her parents. She turned down an offer to sell her business for one and a half million dollars. Is she crazy or a risk taker? In 2004, at the age of fourteen, Ashley Qualls launched the website whateverlife.com as a place to show her portfolio of pictures and graphics. Then she added free MySpace layouts and tutorials for coding and graphic design and hits went through the roof. To help with costs of running the site, she added Google AdSense. Her first check was $2,790; now ad revenue for whateverlife.com brings in more than one million dollars a year. With the site graduating into a social networking community and drawing up to 360,000 hits in a single day, Ashley's risks have paid off (and she finished high school via online courses).[7]

Matt

Kelly Czarnecki is a technology education librarian at ImaginOn for the Public Library of Charlotte & Mecklenburg County in North Carolina. Here she shares a story of a teen who took a positive risk:

> We have a Rock the Mic event one Friday a month. Teens sign up and come into Studio i [our movie/music creation space]. Teens can sing, play music, recite poetry, act, etc. and the teens vote for their favorite performers. One teen, Matt, was really shy and never was interested in performing. He was a "regular" at the library. One day he decided to sign up to perform for Rock the Mic and won first place![9]

Brryan

In December 2009, TeenNick hosted the HALO Awards, given to ordinary teens doing extraordinary things. Stars like Justin Timberlake, Alicia Keys, and LeBron James participated in honoring teens who have taken risks to make their community better. Among the recipients was Brryan Jackson. Living with full-blown AIDS since the age of five, Brryan had an extremely difficult childhood: He often transferred schools in an attempt to avoid the prejudice he suffered from other children (and sometimes the schools themselves). He has gone on to become an active participant in the organization Speak Out, which brings him into schools to give talks and educate students about what it's like living with HIV/AIDS. On his eighteenth birthday, Brryan founded his own organization, Hope Is Vital (HIV), to raise awareness, understanding, and compassion for people infected with and suffering from HIV/AIDS.[8]

These brief examples of teen risk takers all illustrate the benefit that comes from taking a leap. Every teen, or adult, risk may not pay off, but getting into the habit of taking positive risks builds confidence and increases the odds of ultimate success. Librarians can both encourage teens to take positive risks and gain inspiration from the risk-taking teens they encourage. It's possible to use the tips outlined in this book to calculate teen and adult risk levels, garner support for all types of risk taking, and determine which strategies work best for a particular scenario, whether it's a teen or a librarian taking the risk.

NOTES

1. Jill L. Ferguson, "Teens and Risky Behavior," Ezine Articles. com, http://ezinearticles.com/?Teens-and-Risky -Behavior&id=86747.

2. Glenn Greenberg and Deborah Burke Henderson, "Positive Risk Taking Cuts Alcohol and Drug Use among Teens," SADD Teens Today, November 29, 2004, www.sadd.org/ teenstoday/survey04.htm.

3. Ibid.

4. "Risky Behaviors," 4Parents.gov, www.4parents.gov/ sexrisky/risky/risky.html.

5. Tara Kelly, "Plus-Size Supermodel Crystal Renn," *Time*, October 26, 2009, www.time.com/time/arts/ article/0,8599,1931990,00.html.

6. Michelle Garcia, "Crystal Vera's Quest for the Crown," Advocate.com, www.advocate.com/Society/Media/Crystal_ Vera__39;s_quest_for_the_crown.

7. Chuck Salter, "Girl Power," *Fast Company*, September 1, 2007, www.fastcompany.com/magazine/118/girl-power.html.

8. Kelly Czarnecki, interview with Connie Urquhart, December 23, 2009.

9. "The TeenNick HALO Awards: Brryan Jackson," TeenNick, www.teennick.com/halo/winners.php?id=1.

APPENDIX A

Meet the Risk Takers

The librarians listed below helped with this book by telling their risk stories—stories of both success and of failure. Unless otherwise noted, all shared their stories in interviews with the authors.

KELLY CZARNECKI, technology education librarian, ImaginOn, Charlotte, North Carolina
RISKY QUOTE: "It's okay to learn and we don't have to have it right the first time."[1]

MK EAGLE, librarian, Holliston High School (Massachusetts)
RISKY QUOTE: "Going into library sciences (or education, for that matter) is a bit of a risk these days! But I think going out on a limb and working in a historically conservative community, as someone who's pierced and tattooed and very open about my sexuality, is a risk."

BETH GALLAWAY, independent consultant, Information Goddess Consulting, Hampton, New Hampshire
RISKY QUOTE: "I learn by doing, and even if results are not what I expected, I learn, and grow, in the process. Being willing to learn by failing also makes me quick to say yes, try new things, and above all, adapt."

FRANCES JACOBSON HARRIS, librarian, University of Illinois Urbana-Champaign, University Laboratory High School Library
RISKY QUOTE: "For me, the risk taking is in the education piece—trying to teach young people to manage all the input and to make informed choices."

JAMISON HEDIN, librarian, Ludlow High School (Massachusetts)
RISKY QUOTE: "Risk is relative. As professionals and colleagues, I think it's important to think about risks in context and to celebrate them—whether small or large."

ERIN DOWNEY HOWERTON, school liaison, Johnson County Library (Kansas)
RISKY QUOTE: "If we're not speaking up in order to provide patrons with what they want and need, then we're not doing our jobs right—period. Libraries are combination intellectual factories/warehouses and risk is inherent in our work."

SARAH LUDWIG, head of teen and technology services, Darien Library (Connecticut)
RISKY QUOTE: "I took a plunge. I started friending kids. I included a note; you can do this on Facebook. The note said something like: 'Hi, I'm the teen librarian at the Darien Library and I'm trying to get to know people in Darien. I know you don't know me, so if you don't want to accept me as a friend, I totally understand! But if you do, that would be great.'"[2]

RAY LUSK, events coordinator, Madison Library District (Idaho)
RISKY QUOTE: "I firmly believe in taking risks. If you don't take a risk, you have no idea how far you will go or whose life will be changed because of what you do."

KATE PICKETT, young adult librarian, Johnson County Library (Kansas)
RISKY QUOTE: "Sometimes we are taking risks with more than just ourselves."

SARA RYAN, teen services specialist, Multnomah County Library (Oregon)
RISKY QUOTE: "When I think about risks that haven't worked out, the reason for the failure isn't typically in the nature of the risk itself, which is usually around trying something new or changing the way a program works, but rather about the way in which I tried to implement the risk."

STEPHANIE SQUICCIARINI, teen services librarian, Fairport Public Library (New York)
RISKY QUOTE: "I try to find success in whatever I attempt. And I guess I find 'success' a relative term."

NOTES

1.   Kelly Czarnecki, "Learning to Disagree Without Being Disagreeable," YALSA Blog, http://yalsa.ala.org/blog/2008/11/17/learning-to-disagree-without-being-disagreeable.

2. Sarah Ludwig, "The Amazing Power of Facebook," YALSA Blog, http://yalsa.ala.org/blog/2008/11/19/the-amazing-power-of-facebook.

APPENDIX B

Risky Decision Making: Assessing Risk Readiness

Answer the questions below in order to gain insight into your risk-taking readiness.

1. **What experience do you have with risk taking in the workplace? (Select one)**

    ❏ None
    ❏ I've taken one risk before and it was
        ❏ unsuccessful
        ❏ partly successful
        ❏ completely successful
    ❏ I've taken two or more risks before and they were
        ❏ all unsuccessful
        ❏ sometimes a success and sometimes not
        ❏ all completely successful

    If you answered "none," skip to question 5 below.

2. **If you have taken risks previously, list five things that made that risk taking successful or unsuccessful.**

    a. _____

    b. _____

    c. _____

    d. _____

    e. _____

3. **If you are already experienced at risk taking, list five things you would do differently in order to be more successful next time.**

    a. _____

    b. _____

    c. _____

    d. _____

    e. _____

4. **If you are already experienced at risk taking, list five things you would make sure to do exactly the same in order to help guarantee your next risk is as successful or even more successful.**

    a. _____

    b. _____

    c. _____

    d. _____

    e. _____

5. **If you are a novice risk taker, what has held you back from risk taking in the past?**

    ❑   Time
    ❑   Money
    ❑   Administration/colleagues
    ❑   Not knowing how to get started
    ❑   Other. Explain: _____

6. **If you are a novice risk taker, what would make you more comfortable in getting started in taking a risk?**

    ❑   Being able to work with a colleague on the project
    ❑   Knowing that others have taken the same risk before with success
    ❑   Having proof of the same risk being successful for others
    ❑   Having another youth-serving organization approach me to help them take the risk
    ❑   Having administration ask for the risk taking instead of me having to ask to take on a risk
    ❑   Other. Describe: _____

7. Whether you are a novice or experienced risk taker, describe in one paragraph below what you don't like about risk taking.

    _____

    _____

    _____

    _____

8. Whether a novice or experienced risk taker, describe in one paragraph below what you like about risk taking.

    _____

    _____

    _____

    _____

9. Look at how you answered the questions above. Consider what will make a risk-taking endeavor successful for you in your workplace. Then write a paragraph about what the answers above tell you about your own risk-taking abilities and what you want or need in order to be a successful risk taker in the teen library community.

    _____

    _____

    _____

    _____

APPENDIX C

Risky Decision Making
Is This a Risk Worth Taking?

Answer the questions below in order to help you make decisions related to a library risk.

1. **In one or two paragraphs, describe what the project is and how it is risky.**

    _____

    _____

    _____

    _____

2. **What are the goals of the risk taking? (Select as many as apply.)**

    ❏   To improve library services overall to teens in the community
    ❏   To inform and demonstrate to colleagues and administration the importance of teen library services
    ❏   To integrate a brand new program into what's provided to teens in the library
    ❏   To update or upgrade a program or service already provided for teens by the library
    ❏   To give teens an opportunity to be involved in planning and implementing services for them in the library
    ❏   Other. Describe: _____

3. **Who will benefit by the risk taking? (Select all that apply.)**

    ❏   All teens in the community, including those who typically don't come into the library

❑ All teens who are regular visitors to the library
❑ A subset of teens who regularly visit the library
❑ The teen librarian
❑ The library administration and/or colleagues
❑ Staff of other community organization serving youth
❑ Teachers of teens
❑ Parents of teens in the community
❑ Community members
❑ Other. Describe: _____

4. **Describe in one or two paragraphs what the outcome of the risk taking will be in the community and for the groups selected above.**

   _____
   _____
   _____

5. **Does your library have a track record of being risk-friendly?**

   ❑ Yes
   ❑ No
   ❑ Sometimes

6. **If your library is risk-friendly, what five generalizations can you make about the previous risks? For example, did they all come from a particular department or did they all come about because of a specific library partnership?**

   a. _____
   b. _____
   c. _____
   d. _____
   e. _____

7. **If your library is risk-friendly, how many other risky activities are going on at this time?**

   ❑ 1
   ❑ Between 2 and 4
   ❑ 5 or more

8. **If there are one or more risky projects going on currently, will adding another risky activity be one too many?**

   ❑ Yes
   ❑ No

   Explain the reason for answering yes or no above

   _____
   _____
   _____
   _____

9. **If library staff and administration have previously been risk-averse, what five generalizations can be made about that? For example, the director of the library is worried that if something goes wrong, he'll get fired.**

   a. _____
   b. _____
   c. _____
   d. _____
   e. _____

10. **Who presents barriers to the risk taking?** (Select as many as apply.)

    ❑ Administration
    ❑ Colleagues
    ❑ Teachers
    ❑ Staff at other youth-serving agencies
    ❑ Parents
    ❑ Community members as a whole
    ❑ Officials of town/city government
    ❑ Other. Describe: _____

11. **What institutional barriers are in the way of the risk taking?**
    (Select as many as apply.)

    ❑ Time
    ❑ Money

❏ Technology
❏ Overall support from administration and/or colleagues
❏ Other. Describe: _____

12. **What needs to be accomplished before taking the risk that you are thinking about?** (Check as many as apply.)

❏ Talk with teens about the idea and get their feedback
❏ Research in order to find out more about others that have tried this risk and the best and worst practices
❏ Pitch the idea to administrators and/or colleagues
❏ Find others in the community with whom you might partner
❏ Find grants or other funding sources
❏ Other. Describe: _____

13. **What is the one thing that is most frightening about taking this risk and why is it frightening?**

_____
_____
_____
_____

14. **In a paragraph or two, write what the worst thing is that could happen if this risk is taken.**

_____
_____
_____
_____

15. **Look over the information collected above and ask, is this a risk worth taking?** (Select only one.)

❏ Yes, right away
❏ Yes, but it's necessary to do some research and get some backup before getting started
❏ No
❏ Not sure. If not sure, what information do you need in order to make the decision?

Forty Developmental Assets for Adolescents Ages Twelve to Eighteen

EXTERNAL

Support

1. Family support—Family life provides high levels of love and support
2. Positive family communication—Young person and her parent(s) communicate positively, and young person is willing to seek advice and counsel from parents
3. Other adult relationships—Young person receives support from three or more nonparent adults
4. Caring neighborhood—Young person experiences caring neighbors
5. Caring school climate—School provides a caring, encouraging environment
6. Parent involvement in schooling—Parent(s) are actively involved in helping young person succeed in school

Empowerment

7. Community values youth—Young person perceives that adults in the community value youth
8. Youth as resources—Young people are given useful roles in the community
9. Service to others—Young person serves in the community one hour or more per week
10. Safety—Young person feels safe at home, school, and in the neighborhood

Boundaries and Expectations

11. Family boundaries—Family has clear rules and consequences and monitors the young person's whereabouts
12. School boundaries—School provides clear rules and consequences
13. Neighborhood boundaries—Neighbors take responsibility for monitoring young people's behavior
14. Adult role models—Parent(s) and other adults model positive, responsible behavior
15. Positive peer influence—Young person's best friends model responsible behavior
16. High expectations—Both parent(s) and teachers encourage the young person to do well

Constructive Use of Time

17. Creative activities—Young person spends three or more hours per week in lessons or practice in music, theater, or other arts
18. Youth programs—Young person spends three or more hours per week in sports, clubs, or organizations at school and/or in the community
19. Religious community—Young person spends one or more hours per week in activities in a religious institution
20. Time at home—Young person is out with friends "with nothing special to do" two or fewer nights per week

INTERNAL

Commitment to Learning

21. Achievement motivation—Young person is motivated to do well in school
22. School engagement—Young person is actively engaged in learning
23. Homework—Young person reports doing at least one hour of homework every school day
24. Bonding to school—Young person cares about her school
25. Reading for pleasure—Young person reads for pleasure three or more hours per week

Positive Values

26. Caring—Young person places high value on helping other people
27. Equality and social justice—Young person places high value on promoting equality and reducing hunger and poverty
28. Integrity—Young person acts on convictions and stands up for her beliefs
29. Honesty—Young person "tells the truth even when it is not easy"
30. Responsibility—Young person accepts and takes personal responsibility
31. Restraint—Young person believes it is important not to be sexually active or to use alcohol or other drugs

Social Competencies

32. Planning and decision making—Young person knows how to plan ahead and make choices
33. Interpersonal competence—Young person has empathy, sensitivity, and friendship skills
34. Cultural competence—Young person has knowledge of and comfort with people of different cultural/racial/ethnic backgrounds
35. Resistance skills—Young person can resist negative peer pressure and dangerous situations
36. Peaceful conflict resolution—Young person seeks to resolve conflict nonviolently

Positive Identity

37. Personal power—Young person feels he has control over "things that happen to me"
38. Self-esteem—Young person reports having a high self-esteem
39. Sense of purpose—Young person reports that "my life has a purpose"
40. Positive view of personal future—Young person is optimistic about his personal future

Source: The Search Institute, www.search-institute.org/content/40-developmental-assets -adolescents-ages-12-18.

APPENDIX E

Resources That Support
Smart Risk Taking

Materials listed below include resources mentioned in this book, along with other items that can be useful when looking for information on how to be a successful teen librarian risk taker.

LIBRARY AND PUBLISHING BLOGS, JOURNALS, AND WEBSITES

Abel, David. "Welcome to the Library. Say Goodbye to the Books." Boston.com. www.boston.com/news/local/massachusetts/articles/2009/09/04/a_library_without_the_books.

BBC Audiobooks America Blog. "Twitter an Audio Story with Neil Gaiman!" www.bbcaudiobooksamerica.com/TradeHome/Blog/tabid/58/articleType/ArticleView/articleId/110/Twitter-an-Audio-Story-with-Neil-Gaiman.aspx.

Braun, Linda W. "Risk in Teen Services—the Transcript." YALSA Blog. http://yalsa.ala.org/blog/2009/08/06/risk-in-teen-services-the-transcript.

Braun, Linda W. "Risky Business." YALSA Blog. http://yalsa.ala.org/blog/?s=risk.

Eagle, mk. "Not on Facebook—Not Invited?" YALSA Blog. http://yalsa.ala.org/blog/2009/10/15/not-on-facebook-not-invited.

Fister, Barbara. "The Dewey Dilemma." *Library Journal*, October 1, 2009. www.libraryjournal.com/article/CA6698264.html.

Hoffert, Barbara. "Who's Selecting Now?" *Library Journal*, September 1, 2007. www.libraryjournal.com/article/CA6471081.html.

Honig, Megan. "Takin' It to the Street: Teens and Street Lit." *Voice of Youth Advocates* 31, no. 3: 207-11.

Kroski, Ellyssa. "Should Your Library Have a Social Media Policy?" *School Library Journal*, October 1, 2009. www.schoollibraryjournal.com/article/CA6699104.html.

Lesesne, Teri. "Dangerous Minds." YALSA Blog. http://yalsa.ala.org/blog/2009/05/22/dangerous-minds.

Ludwig, Sarah. "The Amazing Power of Facebook." YALSA Blog. http://yalsa.ala.org/blog/2008/11/19/the-amazing-power-of-facebook.

Many Voices. http://twitter.com/manyvoices.

The New York Public Library. "Stuff for the Teen Age 2009." www.nypl.org/books/sta2009/.

Walton, Candace. "Crossing Over: Books from the Other Side." *Voice of Youth Advocates* 32, no. 5 (December 2009): 388–91.

Whalen, Debra Lau. Adolescents Aren't That Stupid After All," *School Library Journal*, January 1, 2007. www.schoollibraryjournal.com/article/CA6403257.html?q=risky+behavior.

YALSA Research Committee. *Current Research Related to Young Adult Services, 2006-2009: A Supplement*, Young Adult Library Services Association. www.ala.org/ala/mgrps/divs/yalsa/research/09researchbibliograp.pdf.

RISKY AUTHORS

Ellen Hopkins. www.ellenhopkins.com.
Barry Lyga. http://barrylyga.com/new.
Lauren Myracle. www.laurenmyracle.com.
Alex Sanchez. www.alexsanchez.com.

RISK RESOURCES

BoardSource. "Managing Risk Can Lead to New Opportunities." www.boardsource.org/Knowledge.asp?ID=1.277.

Center for Informed Decision Making. http://cygnus-group.com/CIDM.

Harris, Robert. "Introduction to Decision Making." VirtualSalt. www.virtualsalt.com/crebook5.htm.

Messina, James J. "Becoming a Risk Taker." LiveStrong.com. www.livestrong.com/article/14727-becoming-a-risk-taker.

Nonprofit Risk Management Center. www.nonprofitrisk.org.

ABOUT YOUTH RISK TAKING AND YOUTH DEVELOPMENT

4Parents.gov. "Risky Behaviors." www.4parents.gov/sexrisky/risky/risky.html.

Ferguson, Jill L. "Teens and Risky Behavior." Ezine@rticles.com.
http://ezinearticles.com/?Teens-and-Risky-Behavior&id=86747.

Garcia, Michelle. "Crystal Vera's Quest for the Crown." Advocate.com.
www.advocate.com/Society/Media/Crystal_Vera__39;s_quest_for_
the_crown.

Greenberg, Glenn and Deborah Burke Henderson. "Positive Risk Taking Cuts
Alcohol and Drug Use Among Teens." SADD Teens Today.
www.sadd.org/teenstoday/survey04.htm.

Kelly, Tara. "Plus-Size Supermodel Crystal Renn." *Time*, October 26, 2009.
www.time.com/time/arts/article/0,8599,1931990,00.html.

Major, Michelle and Kate Escherich. "Plus-Size Model Crystal Renn Gains
Weight and Life." *ABC Good Morning America*, September 8, 2009.
http://abcnews.go.com/GMA/BeautySecrets/size-model-crystal-renn
-gains-weight-finds-success/story?id=8514206&page=1.

Males, Michael. "Does the Adolescent Brain Make Risk Taking Inevitable?"
Journal of Adolescent Research 24 (January 2009) 3–20.

MiddleWeb. "Adolescent Risk-Taking." www.middleweb.com/adolesrisk.html.

Newby, Kara and Anastasia Snyder. *Teen Risk Behaviors.* The Ohio State
University Extension. http://ohioline.osu.edu/hyg-fact/5000/pdf/
5240.pdf.

Salter, Chuck. "Girl Power." *Fast Company*, December 19, 2007.
www.fastcompany.com/magazine/118/girl-power.html.

Search Institute. http://search-institute.org.

TeenNick. "The TeenNick HALO Awards: Brryan Jackson."
www.teennick.com/halo/winners.php?id=1.

Wilkins, Wallace. "Take Risks When There's No Danger." *The Futurist* 33, no.
5 (May 1, 1999): 60.

WhateverLife.com. www.whateverlife.com/about_us.php.

APPENDIX F

YALSA White Papers

WHITE PAPER NO. 1

WHY TEEN SPACE?

KIMBERLY BOLAN, MLS, library consultant
Accepted by the YALSA Board of Directors, June 2007

This paper provides an overview of and commentary on teen space development and its implicit bearing on the strategic vision, planning, and development of facilities design for twenty-first-century libraries. Attention will be drawn to key success factors such as why teen space is important, and current and future priorities and best practices related to library facilities for teenage users. This paper will help you understand the importance of teen space within your community and organization, and address issues that shape the quality of a teen customer's experience with your library.

Background

Over the past twelve years, there has been a transformation in library facility design for teens. Traditionally speaking, common practice has been to ignore dedicated space for teens or to create boring, unfriendly facilities with little attention to adolescent needs and wants. Libraries have generally been designed without teen customers in mind, driven by librarian, administrator, and architect personal likes and ideas. Today more and more schools and public libraries are working to accommodate thirteen- to eighteen-year-olds, moving away from the previously described "traditional" approaches to creating more efficient, innovative, appealing, and teen-inspired spaces.

Position

As libraries continue to move forward, organizations of all types, sizes, and budgets must realize that warm, inviting, comfortable, and user-centered environments are integral in attracting teenage users and transforming the role and image of the library. Such environments are essential in encouraging positive use of libraries for recreational activities, learning, and education.

Whether building a new library, renovating an existing facility, or working on a minor facilities revamp, the primary key success factor is understanding why teen space is critical. Developing dedicated, attractive, motivating, and teen-oriented space provides a way to

- create a positive, safe environment for studying, socializing, and leisure activities
- outwardly and interactively acknowledge teen customers and their needs by supporting adolescent asset development; creating an environment that encourages emotional, social, and intellectual development; and building a sense of teen belonging, community involvement, and library appreciation
- expand your customer base by appealing to users and nonusers, creating a wider variety of customers from diverse social groups, backgrounds, and interests
- effectively market library services by drawing teens into the physical library space, leading them to other library services such as materials, programming, etc.
- increase current and future library supporters: the future of libraries is tomorrow's adults and, believe it or not, these are today's teens

Other key success teen space factors include the following:

- making teen participation and input a priority as well as a regular practice throughout the planning, design, implementation, maintenance, and marketing of the space and related teen library services
- appropriately sizing a teen facility based on a library's community/student population (ages thirteen to eighteen). Libraries must reevaluate space allocations in their overall facilities and scale them according to demographics, not personal bias. In public library

facilities, the ratio of a teen area to the overall library should be equal to the ratio of the teen population of that community to the overall population of that community.

- developing a well-thought-out plan for improvement, including short-term and long-range planning for current and future teen space and services
- getting buy-in and support from all stakeholders, including teens, staff, faculty, administrators, and the community
- creating a truly teen-friendly space that is comfortable, colorful, interactive, flexible in design, and filled with technology. It is important to keep in mind that "teen-friendly" is not synonymous with unruly, unreasonable, impractical, or tacky.
- thinking about what teens need, not about what adults want. Don't make assumptions or let personal biases impact decision making, whether selecting furniture, shelving/displays, flooring, lighting, paint color, signage, etc. Items should be welcoming, have visual impact, be versatile, and encourage positive, independent use of the facility.

Conclusion

Making libraries appealing and important to teens is not an impossible task. Library facilities design is one integral step in attracting teen customers and redefining libraries of the future. Looking at teen facilities design in a new light, letting go of antiquated ideas, reevaluating traditional ways of "doing business," and emphasizing customer needs and wants are essential first steps in moving forward in the world of twenty-first-century libraries.

References

A. Bernier, ed., *Making Space for Teens: Recognizing Young Adult Needs in Library Buildings* (Lanham, MD: Scarecrow Press, forthcoming).

Kimberly Bolan, "Looks Like Teen Spirit," *School Library Journal* 52, no. 1 (November 2006): 44+.

Kimberly Bolan, *Teen Spaces: The Step-by-Step Library Makeover,* 2nd ed. (Chicago: American Library Association, 2009).

Patrick Jones, Mary Kay Chelton, and Joel Shoemaker, *Do It Right: Best Practices for Serving Young Adults in School and Public Libraries* (New York: Neal-Schuman, 2001).

Search Institute, "The 40 Developmental Assets for Adolescents (Ages 12–18)." www.search-institute.org/content/40-developmental-assets-adolescents -ages-12-18.

WHITE PAPER NO. 2

THE VALUE OF YOUNG ADULT LITERATURE

MICHAEL CART

To ask "What is the value of young adult literature?" is to beg at least three other questions:

1. **What is meant by "value"?**
2. **What is meant by "young adult"?**
3. **What is meant by "literature"?**

To answer these questions, in turn

1. **"Value" is defined, simply, as "worth."** When used in juxtaposition with the term "young adult literature," it invites an assessment of how worthwhile, important, or desirable that literature is—measured, as we will see below, in terms both of its aesthetic success and its personal impact on readers and their lives.

2. **"Young adult" is officially defined by YALSA as meaning persons twelve to eighteen years of age.** Unofficially, however, it is acknowledged that "young adult" is an amorphous term that is subject to continuous revision as demanded by changing societal views. Since the early 1990s, for example, it has (again, unofficially) been expanded to include those as young as ten and, since the late 1990s, as old as twenty-five (or even, some would argue, thirty).

3. **"Literature" has traditionally meant published prose—both fiction and nonfiction—and poetry.** The increasing importance of visual communication has begun to expand this definition to include the pictorial as well, especially when offered in combination with text as in the case of picture books, comics, and graphic novels and nonfiction.

Often the word "literature" is also presumed to imply aesthetic merit. However, because young adults have, historically, been accorded such scant respect by society—being viewed more as homogeneous problems than as individual persons—the literature that has been produced for them has, likewise, been dismissed as little more than problem-driven literature of problematic value. Accordingly, the phrase "young adult literature" has itself been dismissed as being an oxymoron.

The Young Adult Library Services Association takes strenuous exception to all of this. Founded in a tradition of respect for those it defines as "young adults," YALSA respects young adult literature as well. A proof of this is the establishment of the Michael L. Printz Award, which YALSA presents annually to the author of the best young adult book of the year, "best" being defined solely in terms of literary merit. In this way, YALSA values young adult literature—*as literature*—for its artistry and its aesthetic integrity.

But to invoke the Printz Award is to invite one last definition: this time of the very phrase "young adult literature," for—like "young adult"—this is an inherently amorphous and dynamic descriptor. Narrowly defined, it means literature specifically published *for* young adults. More broadly, however, it can mean anything that young adults read, though it must—of necessity—have a young adult protagonist and address issues of interest to this readership. This broader definition is demonstrated by YALSA's annual selection of what it calls "Best Books for Young Adults," a list that often includes books published for adults and even, sometimes, for children.

Whether young adult literature is defined narrowly or broadly, however, much of its value is to be found in how it addresses the needs of its readers. Often described as "developmental," these books acknowledge that young adults are beings in evolution, in search of self and identity; beings who are constantly growing and changing, morphing from the condition of childhood to that of adulthood. That period of passage called "young adulthood" is a unique part of life, distinguished by unique needs that are—at minimum—physical, intellectual, emotional, and societal in nature. By addressing these needs, young adult literature is made valuable not only by its artistry but also by its relevance to the lives of its readers. And by addressing not only their needs but also their interests, the literature becomes a powerful inducement for them to read, another compelling reason to value it.

Yet another of the chief values of young adult literature is to be found in its capacity to offer readers an opportunity to see themselves reflected in its pages. Young adulthood is, intrinsically, a period of tension. On the one hand, young adults have an all-consuming need to belong. But on the other, they are also inherently solipsistic, regarding themselves as being unique, which is not cause for celebration but, rather, for despair. For to be unique is to be unlike one's peers, to be "other," in fact. And to be "other" is to not belong but, instead, to be an outcast. Thus, to see oneself in the pages of a young adult book is to receive the blessed reassurance that one is not alone after all, not other, not alien, but, instead, a viable part of a larger community of beings who share a common humanity.

Another value of young adult literature is its capacity to foster understanding, empathy, and compassion by offering vividly realized portraits of the lives—exterior and interior—of individuals who are *un*like the reader. In this way, young adult literature invites its readership to embrace the humanity it shares with those who—if not for the encounter in reading—might forever remain strangers or—worse—irredeemably "other."

Still another value of young adult literature is its capacity for telling its readers the truth, however disagreeable that may sometimes be; for in this way, it equips readers for dealing with the realities of impending adulthood and—though it may sound quaintly old-fashioned—for assuming the rights and responsibilities of citizenship.

By giving readers such a frame of reference, it also helps them to find role models, to make sense of the world they inhabit, to develop a personal philosophy of being, to determine what is right and, equally, what is wrong, and to cultivate a personal sensibility. To, in other words, become civilized.

So what, finally, is the value of young adult literature? One might as well ask, "What is the value of breathing?"—for both are essential, even fundamental, to life and survival.

WHITE PAPER NO. 3

THE BENEFITS OF INCLUDING DEDICATED YOUNG ADULT LIBRARIANS ON STAFF IN THE PUBLIC LIBRARY

AUDRA CAPLAN with the Young Adult Library Services Association

Background

The Young Adult Library Services Association adopted a strategic plan in 2004. That plan included a core purpose and a vivid description of the desired future. The core purpose is "to advocate for excellence in library services to the teen population." The first bullet below the description states: "There will be a young adult librarian in every public and secondary school library." The group of practitioners who developed both of these statements understood that advocating excellence in library service for teens goes hand in hand with the provision of a dedicated young adult librarian in each location that serves teens.

Position

Why is it important to have young adult librarians on staff?

Because a significant percent of the American population is composed of adolescents and many of them are library users. There are over thirty million teens currently in the United States, the largest generation since the baby boomers, and, according to a 2007 survey of young people conducted by a Harris Poll for the Young Adult Library Services Association, 78 percent of these teen respondents have library cards. Not surprisingly, participation in library programs by youth under age eighteen has been rising steadily over the past decade, from 35.5 million per year in 1993 to more than 51.8 million in 2001. We also know that while 14.3 million kindergarteners through twelfth graders are home alone after school every day, three-quarters of Americans believe it is a high priority for public libraries to offer a safe place where teens can study and congregate. Unfortunately, many communities do not provide after-school or weekend activities that can engage teens, despite the understanding that successful, well-prepared young adults are essential to fill roles as contributing members of a vital society, and that teens need responsive and responsible venues in which to develop into successful, contributing members of society.

Why can't generalist library staff serve the teen population as well as young adult librarians?

Because librarians especially trained to work with young adults are age-level specialists who understand that teens have unique needs and who have been trained especially to work with this particular population. As books like Barbara Strauch's *The Primal Teen: What New Discoveries about the Teenage Brain Tell Us about Our Kids* have shown us, teens' brains and bodies are different from a child's or an adult's. As a result, their behavior, interests, and informational and social needs are not the same as those of children or adults.

The Chapin Hall Center for Children completed a study in 2004 on "Teens in the Library." In the area of staffing, the first statement related to improving youth services in libraries is that "dedicated staff are essential to effective youth programs." Across all of the sites studied by Chapin Hall and the Urban Institute, senior administrators and librarians agreed that "youth programs require a staff person whose priority is to manage the program. . . ." Library services that best address teen needs and interests are the professional priority of young adult librarians.

Why provide staff and services specifically for teens?

Dedicated library services for teens improve the library as a whole. Armed with knowledge and understanding of adolescent behavior, interests, and needs, young adult librarians create programming and build collections appropriate to the concerns of young adults and develop services based on knowledge of adolescent development. They are experts in the field of young adult literature and keep up with current teen trends in reading, technology, education, and popular culture. They provide reference services that help young adults find and use information, and they promote activities that build and strengthen information literacy skills. They know the benefits of youth participation and understand it is essential to the offer of excellent service to teens, encouraging teens to provide direct input to library service through activities such as teen advisory groups and volunteer or paid work in libraries. They also collaborate with other youth development experts in the community and with agencies that provide services to teens.

According to key findings from the Wallace Foundation's "Public Libraries as Partners in Youth Development (PLPYD)," public libraries selected for this program were challenged to "develop or expand youth programs that engaged individual teens in a developmentally supportive manner while enhancing library services for all youth in the community." Based on the experiences of the PLPYD sites, the findings conclude that "Public libraries have the potential to design youth programs that provide developmentally enriching experiences to teens and have positive effect both on youth services and the library more broadly."

Young adult librarians build relationships with teens and help other staff to feel comfortable with them. One of the findings from a study by Chapin Hall indicated that staff prejudice in relation to teens broke down when staff can be mentored to develop relationships with teens. Youth development principles were credited with changing the general culture of the library by providing an "important new language" for library administrators that helped the library to establish a new leadership role in the area of youth development and in the community. In an era when libraries must clearly articulate their importance to the larger community, the role of youth development agency increases the public library's value as an institution and also makes good economic sense for the community.

A 2007 survey conducted by the Harris Poll for YALSA asked young people what needed to happen in their local library in order for them to use it more often. One in five respondents said they would use their library more if "there was a librarian just for teens." One-third of respondents said that they would use the library more if the library had more interesting materials to borrow and events to attend.

The young adult librarian acts as a significant adult in the lives of many young people, thereby meeting one of the Search Institute's developmental needs of teens: positive social interaction with peers and adults.

Conclusion

Why employ young adult librarians?

The practical reasons are listed above. On a fundamental level, the goal is to provide excellent service to a large but unique segment of the population: teens. Young adult librarians are essential to providing the best service to young adults in libraries, and they are essential to keeping libraries viable and up-to-date by translating knowledge about cultural trends into programs, collections, staff engagement with youth, and collaborative efforts in the broader community. So the answer is simple—employing young adult librarians is the smart thing to do.

References

Afterschool Alliance, "7 in 10 Voters Want New Congress to Increase Funding for Afterschool Programs, Poll Finds," November 13, 2006 press release.

Americans for Libraries Council, "Learning in Motion: A Sampling of Library Teen Programs." www.publicagenda.org/files/research_facts/long_overdue_teens_fact_sheet.pdf.

Chapin Hall Center for Children, "New on the Shelf: Teens in the Library." www.chapinhall.org/research/report/new-shelf.

Harris Interactive, Inc., "American Library Association: Youth and Library Use Study." www.ala.org/ala/mgrps/divs/yalsa/HarrisYouthPoll.pdf.

Patrick Jones, *New Directions for Library Service to Young Adults* (Chicago: American Library Association/Young Adult Library Services Association, 2003).

Public Agenda, "Long Overdue: A Fresh Look at Public and Leadership
    Attitudes about Libraries in the 21st Century." www.publicagenda.org/
    files/pdf/Long_Overdue.pdf.

Public Library Association, *2007 PLDS Statistical Report* (Chicago: PLA, 2007).

Roxanne Spillett, "When School Day Ends, Danger Begins for the Young,"
    Atlanta Journal-Constitution, October 3, 2002.

Barbara Strauch, *The Primal Teen: What New Discoveries about the Teenage Brain
    Tell Us about Our Kids* (New York: Doubleday, 2003).

Wallace Foundation, "Public Libraries as Partners in Youth
    Development (PLPYD)." www.wallacefoundation.org/
    GrantsPrograms/FocusAreasPrograms/Libraries/Pages/
    PublicLibrariesasPartnersinYouthDevelopment.aspx.

YALSA, "Competencies for Librarians Serving Youth: Young Adults
    Deserve the Best." www.ala.org/ala/mgrps/divs/yalsa/profdev/
    youngadultsdeserve.cfm.

WHITE PAPER NO. 4

THE IMPORTANCE OF YOUNG ADULT SERVICES IN LIS CURRICULA

DON LATHAM, on behalf of the Young Adult Library Services Association

Abstract

This white paper discusses the importance of educational programs for training young adult librarians within schools of library and information science (LIS). It describes the evolution of library services to young adults as well as education for young adult librarians. It identifies the various competencies needed by young adult librarians in the twenty-first century and situates these competencies within the larger context of LIS curricula. Finally, it concludes by emphasizing the value of young adult library services courses both for professionals-in-training and for young adults.

Background

American libraries have a long and proud tradition of providing services to young adults (defined by the Young Adult Library Services Association as young people ages twelve to eighteen). The Brooklyn Youth Library opened in Brooklyn, New York, in 1823, nearly seventy-five years before psychologist G. Stanley Hall introduced the concept of "adolescence" into the popular parlance. In the twentieth century, the profession saw a burgeoning in young adult services in libraries, particularly in the period following World War II. As a result, in 1957 the American Library Association established the Young Adult Services Division (now the Young Adult Library Services Association) as a separate entity from the Children's Library Association. Over the years, the profession has produced a number of outstanding librarians and advocates for young adult services, among them Margaret Edwards, the young people's librarian at Enoch Pratt Free Library in Baltimore, and Michael Printz, a school librarian in Topeka, Kansas, both of whom now have young adult book awards named for them.

Concomitant with this growth in library services for young adults has been a growth in programs for educating young adult librarians. Some of the earliest of these included the Pratt Institute in Brooklyn, Case Western in Cleveland, and the Carnegie Library of Pittsburgh's Training School for Children's Librarians. Now most schools of library and information science offer at least one course in young adult resources and/or services, and many offer multiple courses. A search of the Association for Library and Information Science Education (ALISE) membership directory reveals that approximately 13 percent of ALISE members identify "young adult services" as one of their teaching and/ or research areas.

And, indeed, the need for young adult services in libraries is greater than ever before. According to the U.S. Census Bureau, the number of young people ages ten to nineteen increased from approximately thirty-five million in 1990 to over forty million in 2000 and to nearly forty-two million by 2007. In addition to the increasing numbers of young adults, there has been an explosion in information technologies, a proliferation of resource formats (and user preferences), and a growing emphasis on the importance of information literacy, all of which have presented both exciting opportunities and formidable challenges for librarians who serve young adults.

Position

The Young Adult Library Services Association (YALSA) is committed to the philosophy that "young adults deserve the best." Recognizing the varied knowledge and skill sets needed to provide exemplary services to young adults in the twenty-first century, the division works to promote a rich and diverse educational experience for students preparing to become young adult librarians as well as other information professionals who will work, at least in part, with young adults.

Toward that end, in 2003 the division adopted a set of core competencies for young adult librarians, in which seven areas of competency are identified: leadership and professionalism, knowledge of client group, communication, administration, knowledge of materials, access to information, and services. LIS schools can foster these competencies through various means: by offering courses devoted specifically to young adult resources, services, and programming; by incorporating discussion of young adult users and their information needs into other courses, such as reference services, media production, research methods, and information policy; and by encouraging students to gain valuable experiences outside of the classroom, through such things as internships in young adult services and membership in professional associations like YALSA and the American Association of School Librarians.

The most important competency, because it is that from which the other competencies follow, is knowledge of young adults, and LIS curricula should incorporate that topic into various courses. Knowledge of young adults includes understanding the developmental needs of teens and recognizing that these needs can be different for different teens. It also includes an understanding of the diversity among teens and an appreciation of the information needs of teens from various cultural and ethnic backgrounds. And it involves a recognition of the special needs of "extreme teens," that is, those teens who do not fit the mold of the "typical teen" perhaps because of their educational situation, their living situation, and/or their sexuality. Knowledge of young adult users and their information needs is complemented by an understanding of how to conduct user needs assessment, so research methods should be an integral part of education for young adult librarianship.

LIS curricula should also provide education in the myriad resources that are available to today's young adults. Libraries traditionally have promoted reading, and that is still a core mission. But it is also the case that teens now engage with various forms of media in addition to print: movies, television, games (especially computer games), music, and, of course, the Internet. Young adult librarians should be conversant with the seemingly infinite variety of materials now available in order to meet the needs and preferences of the clients they serve.

Today's young adults are not only consumers of media, but also producers. Most are avid computer users, engaging in social networking, creating their own digital videos, participating in gaming, texting, instant messaging—and often doing several of these things at once! Young adult librarians certainly should be trained in the use of information technology to create and deliver information services, but they should also be educated to understand the broader cultural implications of how and why teens use technology and how this is changing the way teens interact with and process information.

Closely related to the use of technology as a way of accessing and interacting with information is the concept of information literacy. Young adult librarians should be educated to understand what information literacy is and how to promote information literacy skill development among teens. Information literacy—which may be defined as the ability to access, evaluate, and use information ethically and effectively—has received much attention both in the K–12 and higher education environments in the twenty-first century. (See, for example, the standards developed by the American Association of School Librarians 1998 and the Association of College and Research Libraries 2000.) Such skills are seen as increasingly necessary for success in school, the workplace, and life. The teenage years are a crucial time in the acquisition of the numerous complex skills related to information literacy, and young adult librarians can play an important role in ensuring that teens are successful in developing these abilities.

Designing effective programs to promote resources, technology, and information literacy among teens provides a way to bring together these three pillars of young adult services. LIS schools should offer courses in various types of programming as well as the marketing of services to teens. After all, today's teenaged library users will become tomorrow's adult library users—and, hopefully, library supporters. Some will even become tomorrow's librarians.

Conclusion

For these reasons, the Young Adult Library Services Association affirms the value and importance of young adult services in LIS curricula. Educating young adult librarians for the twenty-first century represents a commitment to helping young adults become lifelong readers, lifelong learners, and lifelong library users.

References

AASL/AECT, *Information Power: Building Partnerships for Learning* (Chicago: American Library Association, 1998).

S. B. Anderson, *Extreme Teens: Library Services to Nontraditional Young Adults* (Westport, CT: Libraries Unlimited, 2005).

Association of College and Research Libraries, "Information Literacy Competency Standards for Higher Education." www.ala.org/ala/mgrps/divs/acrl/standards/informationliteracycompetency.cfm.

Association for Library and Information Science Education (ALISE), "Directory of LIS Programs and Faculty in the United States and Canada—2007." www.alise.org/mc/page.do?sitePageId=55644&orgId=ali.

A. Bernier, M. K. Chelton, C. A. Jenkins, and J. B. Pierce, "Two Hundred Years of Young Adult Library Services History," *Voice of Youth Advocates* 28: 106–11.

C. A. Jenkins, "The History of Youth Services Librarianship: A Review of the Research Literature," *Libraries and Culture* 35: 103–40.

P. Jones, M. Gorman, and T. Suellentrop, *Connecting Young Adults and Libraries: A How-to-Do-It Manual for Librarians*, 3rd ed. (New York: Neal-Schuman, 2004).

U.S. Census Bureau, "Resident Population by Age and Sex. The 2009 Statistical Abstract." www.census.gov/compendia/statab/cats/population/estimates_and_projections_by_age_sex_raceethnicity.html.

Young Adult Library Services Association (YALSA), "Young Adults Deserve the Best: Competencies for Librarians Serving Young Adults." www.ala.org/ala/mgrps/divs/yalsa/profdev/yacompetencies/competencies.cfm.

Young Adult Library Services Association (YALSA), "Who Was Mike Printz?" www.ala.org/ala/mgrps/divs/yalsa/booklistsawards/printzaward/whowasmikeprintz/whomikeprintz.cfm.

APPENDIX G

Young Adults Deserve the Best
YALSA's Competencies for Librarians Serving Youth

AREA I.
Leadership and Professionalism

The librarian will be able to:

Develop and demonstrate leadership skills in identifying the unique needs of young adults and advocating for service excellence, including equitable funding and staffing levels relative to those provided for adults and children.

Develop and demonstrate a commitment to professionalism and ethical behavior.

Plan for personal and professional growth and career development.

Encourage young adults to become lifelong library users by helping them to discover what libraries offer, how to use library resources, and how libraries can assist them in actualizing their overall growth and development.

Develop and supervise formal youth participation, such as teen advisory groups, recruitment of teen volunteers, and opportunities for employment.

Model commitment to building assets in youth in order to develop healthy, successful young adults.

Implement mentoring methods to attract, develop, and train staff working with young adults.

AREA II.
Knowledge of Client Group

The librarian will be able to:

Become familiar with the developmental needs of young adults in order to provide the most appropriate resources and services.

Keep up to date with popular culture and technological advances that interest young adults.

Demonstrate an understanding of, and a respect for, diverse cultural, religious, and ethnic values.

Identify and meet the needs of patrons with special needs.

AREA III.
Communication, Marketing, and Outreach

The librarian will be able to:

Form appropriate professional relationships with young adults, providing them with the assets, inputs, and resiliency factors that they need to develop into caring, competent adults.

Develop relationships and partnerships with young adults, administrators, and other youth-serving professionals in the community by establishing regular communication and by taking advantage of opportunities to meet in person.

Be an advocate for young adults and effectively promote the role of the library in serving young adults, demonstrating that the provision of services to this group can help young adults build assets, achieve success, and in turn, create a stronger community.

Design, implement, and evaluate a strategic marketing plan for promoting young adult services in the library, schools, youth-serving agencies, and the community at large.

Demonstrate the capacity to articulate relationships between young adult services and the parent institution's core goals and mission.

Establish an environment in the library wherein all staff serve young adults with courtesy and respect, and all staff are encouraged to promote programs and services for young adults.

Identify young adult interests and groups underserved or not yet served by the library, including at-risk teens, those with disabilities, non–English speakers, etc., as well as those with special or niche interests.

Promote young adult library services directly to young adults through school visits, library tours, etc., and through engaging their parents, educators, and other youth-serving community partners.

AREA IV.
Administration

The librarian will be able to:

Develop a strategic plan for library service with young adults based on their unique needs.

Design and conduct a community analysis and needs assessment.

Apply research findings towards the development and improvement of young adult library services.

Design activities to involve young adults in planning and decision-making.

Develop, justify, administer, and evaluate a budget for young adult services.

Develop physical facilities dedicated to the achievement of young adult service goals.

Develop written policies that mandate the rights of young adults to equitable library service.

Design, implement, and evaluate an ongoing program of professional development for all staff, to encourage and inspire continual excellence in service to young adults.

Identify and defend resources (staff, materials, facilities, funding) that will improve library service to young adults.

Document young adult programs and activities so as to contribute to institutional and professional memory.

Develop and manage services that utilize the skills, talents, and resources of young adults in the school or community.

AREA V.
Knowledge of Materials

The librarian will be able to:

Meet the informational and recreational needs of young adults through the development of an appropriate collection for all types of readers and non-readers.

Develop a collection development policy that supports and reflects the needs and interests of young adults and is consistent with the parent institution's mission and policies.

Demonstrate a knowledge and appreciation of literature for and by young adults in traditional and emerging formats.

Develop a collection of materials from a broad range of selection sources, and for a variety of reading skill levels, that encompasses all appropriate formats, including, but not limited to, media that reflect varied and emerging technologies, and materials in languages other than English.

Serve as a knowledgeable resource to schools in the community as well as parents and caregivers on materials for young adults.

AREA VI.
Access to Information

The librarian will be able to:

Organize physical and virtual collections to maximize easy, equitable, and independent access to information by young adults.

Utilize current merchandising and promotional techniques to attract and invite young adults to use the collection.

Provide access to specialized information (i.e., community resources, work by local youth, etc.).

Formally and informally instruct young adults in basic research skills, including how to find, evaluate, and use information effectively.

Be an active partner in the development and implementation of technology and electronic resources to ensure young adults' access to knowledge and information.

Maintain awareness of ongoing technological advances and how they can improve access to information for young adults.

AREA VII.
Services

The librarian will be able to:

Design, implement, and evaluate programs and services within the framework of the library's strategic plan and based on the developmental needs of young adults and the public assets libraries represent, with young adult involvement whenever possible.

Identify and plan services with young adults in nontraditional settings, such as hospitals, home-school settings, alternative education, foster care programs, and detention facilities.

Provide a variety of informational and recreational services to meet the diverse needs and interests of young adults and to direct their own personal growth and development.

Continually identify trends and pop-culture interests of young people to inform, and direct their recreational collection and programming needs.

Instruct young adults in basic information gathering, research skills, and information literacy skills—including those necessary to evaluate and use electronic information sources—to develop life-long learning habits.

Actively involve young adults in planning and implementing services and programs for their age group through advisory boards, task forces, and by less formal means (i.e., surveys, one-on-one discussion, focus groups, etc.)

Create an environment that embraces the flexible and changing nature of young adults' entertainment, technological and informational needs.

INDEX

A

administrators
  developing relationships with,
    79–80, 93
  fear of reactions of, 16
  meeting with teen advisory
    board, 54, 58
  and programming, 46, 47, 58
adult material in teen collection,
  20–21
adult role models, 5
after-school organizations as
  partners, 56
age of user in collection
  development policy, 27
anecdotes in proposals, 83
arrangement of collection, 21–22,
  23
audience building, 46, 48, 49–51
audience for pitch for project, 81
author interviews
  Ellen Hopkins, 35–37
  Barry Lyga, 37–40
  Lauren Myracle, 40–42
  Alex Sanchez, 42–44

B

baby steps in programming, 47, 57
beta period and minimizing risk,
  11–12, 85
blogging, 64
book discussion groups on Web, 68
book festivals, 56
book trailers, 68
booklists
  containing titles for adults, 21
  vs. personal recommendation, 25
  Web-based versions, 70
bookstore-like arrangement of
  collection, 21–22
booktalking using Web-based book
  trailers, 68
boundaries and expectations
  (developmental assets), 5
branding of programming, 59
Braun, Linda W., 87–90

break dancing workshops, 55
browsing, 21–22
Burns, Liz, 61
buzz, building of, among staff, 80

C
career development (case studies)
  Linda W. Braun, 87–90
  Jack Martin, 91–95
  Connie Urquhart, 95–97
caring school climate, 32
Cart, Michael, 2–4
case studies in proposals, 83
challenges to materials, 28
change
  in career development, 92–93
  and collection development, 33
  fears of, 86
  and need for innovation and new
    services, 11
child sexual abuse, books on, 35–37
collaboration with other
    organizations. *See* partnerships
collaborative technologies, 65–67
collection development, 15–34
  adult material in, 20–21
  arrangement of collection, 21–22
  and community needs, 22–23
  controversial materials, 4, 17–19,
    28, 30–32
  digital resources, 26–27
  outsourcing, 22–24
  policies for, 27–28, 29, 30
  profile: Beth Gallaway, 18
  readers' advisory, 24–25
  review sources, 19–20
  risks in, 16–17
  weeding, 25–26

communications
  with administrators, 79–80, 93
  collection development policy on
    library website, 28
  with library staff, 48, 57–58,
    79–80
  in risk management, 9
community
  anticipation of reactions, 16, 85
  gauging temperament of, 31–32,
    46, 47
  informing about importance of
    teen materials, 33
  support for library put at risk by
    teen services, 7–8
community needs and collection
    development, 22–23, 24
community organizations as source
    of program presenters, 56
community risks for teens, 100
controversial issues in
    programming, 31, 39–40, 48
controversial materials, 4, 17–19, 28,
    30–32
costs in project proposals, 82–83, 84
craft activities, 53
creating writing groups online,
    69–70
curriculum-based nonfiction,
    substitution of databases for,
    27
Czarnecki, Kelly, 103, 105

D
demand as selection criterion, 18
Developmental Assets for
    Adolescents
  and collections, 32–33

list of, 117–119

teens learning to take risks, 5

developmental processes of teens

and learning to use social media, 65

and need for full access to
Internet, 72–73

and risks for teens, 100

digital resources, 26–27

discomfort with technology, 71

displays *vs.* personal
recommendations, 25

E

Eagle, mk, 17, 74, 105

evaluation of project in proposal, 83

evaluation of risk checklist, 113–116

extreme programming, building
track record for, 48–49

F

face-to-face interactions, alternatives
to, 71

See also one-on-one interactions

fear of failure, 10, 15–16, 97

feedback from users and minimizing
risk, 11–12

filtering, 72–74

flexibility

in collection development policy,
28

in services to YAs, 4

formats, alternative, in
programming, 48

friending teens, 62–64

Friends groups as funding sources,
85

funding sources, finding, 84–85

fundraising, timing of, 81–82

G

Gallaway, Beth, 18, 20, 105

gaming, 18, 20, 55, 101

gay teens, 7

See also LGBTQ materials

Gay-Straight Alliances, 50

genres in collection development
policy, 27

Google Docs, 65, 66

grants, 59

graphic novels, 30

H

Harris, Frances Jacobson, 61, 63–64,
105

headlines for programs, 59

Hedin, Jamison, 16–17, 31, 65, 105

homeless teens and programming,
50

homework help services, 27, 101

homosexual themes. *See* LGBTQ
materials

Honig, Megan, 20–21

Hopkins, Ellen, 35–37

Howerton, Erin Downey, 15, 33, 106

I

improv comedy programs, 53

inaction, results of, 97

information literacy instruction on
library Web page, 69

innovation, lack of, 10–11

Internet safety, instruction in, 72–74

J

Jackson, Brryan, 103

jobs, leaving of, as risk, 88–89,
91–92

K

Kroski, Ellyssa, 64–65

L

labeling, resistance to, 15
LGBTQ materials, 17–19, 30
   See also gay teens
library building, going outside of
   school visits, 52
   teen gathering places, 50
library education (YALSA white
   paper), 134–138
library lock-in programs, 55
library staff
   and collaborative technologies,
      65–66
   developing relationships with,
      79–80
   fear of reactions of, 16
   opposition to teen services, 7–8
   support for programming, 48,
      57–58
life risks for teens, 100
limits, acknowledgment of, 46
long-range plans of library and
   developing support, 79
long-term thinking, 8
Ludwig, Sarah, 62–63, 106
Lusk, Ray, 50–51, 51–53, 106
Lyga, Barry, 37–40

M

machinima design workshops, 55
Many Voices project, 69–70
Martin, Jack, 91–95
mature materials in teen collection, 21
media, promotion of programs on,
   58–59

mentors, 80–81, 96
mission of library, 79
mistakes, learning from, 12–13
mobility in career development,
   91–92
Myracle, Lauren, 40–42

N

naysayers, developing relationships
   with, 79–80
nonusers, programming for, 49–51
   See also users only outside the
      library

O

offensive language. *See* controversial
   materials
off-site users. *See* users only outside
   the library
one-on-one interactions
   finding more time for, 24
   and personal recommendations,
      25
   See also face-to-face interactions,
      alternatives to
outsourcing, 22–24

P

parents, fear of reactions of, 16
partnerships
   and access to funding sources, 85
   and documentation of success, 59
   for programming, 51–53, 56–57
passion and excitement in proposals,
   83
peer pressure, 6
perception of project in community, 85

perception of risk *vs.* reality, 9–10, 31, 39–40

   See also evaluation of risk checklist

permissions for publication, 59

personal power enhanced by library resources, 33

personal recommendations, 24–25

Pickett, Kate, 30, 54–55, 106

politics in libraries, 93

popularity as selection criterion, 18

positivity in developing support, 78

preparation for presentation of proposal, 84–86

presentations for proposing a project, 82, 84

privacy settings on social networks, 63

profanity as controversial topic, 30

programming, 45–60

   audience for, 49–51

   best practices, 53–55

   extreme programs, 55–56

   interview: Ray Lusk, 51–53

   moving forward with, 47–49

   partnerships, 56–57

   preparation for, 45–46

   support for, 57–59

project development

   and budgeting, 82–83

   and building relationships, 79–80

   enthusiasm for, 78, 83

   and mentors, 80–81

   and mission of library, 79

   preparation for presentation, 84–86

   and success stories, 83

   target audience for, 81

   and timing of presentation, 81–82

project management for teens' ideas, 54

promotion of programs, 58–59

Q

Qualls, Ashley, 102

R

racism as controversial topic, 30

readers' advisory services, 24–25

reading for pleasure, 32

Renn, Crystal, 101–102

resources webliography, 121–123

responsibility for one's actions as developmental asset, 5

return on investment in proposals, 85

review sources

   in collection development policy, 27

   for controversial topics, 30–31

   nontraditional resources, 19–20

risk assessment, 7–9

risk avoidance, 8–9

risk checklists

   evaluation of risk, 113–116

   for risk readiness, 109–111

   use of, 56

risk management techniques, 9, 11–12, 96–97

risks, overview of, 1–13

   and innovation, 10–11

   management of, 9, 11–12

   as part of the job, 1–2, 6–7

   perceived *vs.* actual, 9–10, 31, 39–40

   in teens' lives, 3, 5–6, 100–101

Ryan, Sara, 80, 106

S

Sanchez, Alex, 42–44

school risks for teens, 100

Search Institute, Forty
    Developmental Assets, 5–6,
    32–33, 117–119

selection criteria in collection
    development policy, 27

self-censorship, 33

senior centers as opportunity for
    teen volunteers, 56

sexuality, information on, 6

sexually explicit content, 30, 38
    See also controversial materials

shelving in multiple locations, 22

social networking
    and book discussion groups, 68
    library as only place to find
        answer, 6
    policies and guidelines for, 64–65
    promotion of programs on,
        58–59

Squicciarini, Stephanie, 56, 106

statistics, uses of, 71

storytelling in proposals, 83

strategic plan and developing
    support, 79

street and urban lit in collection, 21

success, celebration of, 55

success, documentation of, 59

suicide as controversial topic, 30

summer reading programs for teens,
    51–53

support for programming, 57–58

support for projects, developing. *See*
    project development

T

taboo subjects. *See* controversial
    issues

talent shows, 101

technology in programs and
    services, 61–75
    benefits of, 65–67, 74–75
    as extensions of existing
        services, 67–70
    filtering, 72–74
    and off-site services, 70–72
    policies for social media, 64–65
    time-frame for implementation,
        82

teen advisory board
    advice on collection management,
        26
    for developing life skills, 101
    meeting with administrators, 54,
        58
    programming, 53–55
    selection of materials by, 23

teen prostitution, 36

teen spaces (YALSA white paper),
    125–128

teens
    as future library advocates, 4
    as resources for promotion of
        collection, 32
    risk in lives of, 3, 5–6, 100–101
    as role models, 99–104
    support from for programming,
        58

teens as role models (case studies)
    entrepreneur, 102
    HIV/AIDS activist, 103
    performer, 102
    transgendered teen, 102

timing of pitch for project, 81–82

Twitter, 95–96

U

urban and street lit in collection, 12

Urquhart, Connie, 95–97

users only outside the library, 62–63, 65, 66, 70–72

V

Vera, Crystal, 102

volunteers, use of, 85

W

Waters, Jen, 30

weeding, 25–26, 28

wikis, 65, 66

Y

YALSA Best Books for Young Adults, 18

YALSA Quick Picks list as review source, 18–19

YALSA selected resources lists, 18–19

YALSA white papers

Benefits of…Young Adult Librarians on Staff, 130–134

Importance of Young Adult Services in LIS Curricula, 134–138

Value of Young Adult Literature, 128–130

Why Teen Space?, 125–128

young adult librarians and librarianship

as advocates for teens, 6–7, 54–55

competencies for, 130–143

current situation of, 2–3

forces against, 2

as risk, 3, 5

YALSA white paper, 130–134

young adult literature

trends, 4

YALSA white paper, 128–130

You may also be interested in

Young Adults Deserve the Best: The first book to thoroughly expand on YALSA's "Young Adults Deserve the Best: Competencies for Librarians Serving Youth," this useful resource includes anecdotes and success stories from the field, guidelines which can be used to create evaluation instruments, determine staffing needs, and develop job descriptions, and additional professional resources following each chapter that will help librarians turn theory into practice.

Multicultural Programs for Tweens and Teens: A one-stop resource that encourages children and young adults to explore different cultures, this book includes dozens of flexible programming ideas which allow you to choose a program specific to your scheduling needs; create an event that reflects a specific culture; and recommend further resources to tweens and teens interested in learning more about diverse cultures.

Quick and Popular Reads for Teens: This resource compiles bibliographic information about the books honored by YALSA's *Popular Paperbacks for Young Adults* and *Quick Picks for Reluctant Readers*. Make choosing titles for teens fun, quick, and easy with this one-of-a-kind resource!

A Year of Programs for Teens 2: This volume offers several new themed book lists and read-alikes as well as appendices with reproducible handouts for the various programs. Also included is a section of introductory material that includes general programming advice, information on teen clubs, and marketing ideas, and more than 30 programs cleverly organized around a calendar year, including several that focus on technology, with many other ideas that can adapted year-round as needed.

Order today at www.alastore.ala.org or 866-746-7252!

ALA Store purchases fund advocacy, awareness, and accreditation programs for library professionals worldwide.

CPSIA information can be obtained at www.ICGtesting.com
Printed in the USA
LVOW091451150612

286341LV00009B/49/P